Wine and Beer Making

Derek Watkins

David & Charles
Newton Abbot   London
North Pomfret (Vt)   Vancouver

British Library Cataloguing in Publication Data

Watkins, Derek
    Wine and beer making – (David & Charles leisure and travel series).
    1. Wine and wine making – Amateurs' manuals
    I. Title
    641.8'72   TP548.2

ISBN 0-7153-7503-2

Typeset by Tradespools Limited, Frome
and printed in Great Britain by
Redwood Burn Limited, Trowbridge & Esher
for David & Charles (Publishers) Limited
Brunel House   Newton Abbot   Devon

Published in the United States of America
by David & Charles Inc
North Pomfret   Vermont 05053 . USA

Published in Canada
by Douglas David & Charles Limited
1875 Welch Street   North Vancouver   BC

Widen Your Horizons with this Series

Remember that we cater for all interests. See for yourself with our varied list of titles.

Places to see

Scottish Islands – Tom Weir
Dartmoor – Crispin Gill

Leisure activities

Good Photography Made Easy – Derek Watkins
Cine Photography Made Easy – Derek Watkins
Looking at Churches – David Bowen
Railways for Pleasure – Geoffrey Body
Brass and Other Rubbings – Emma Wood
The Antique-Hunter's Handbook – Ronald Rawlings

Sporting

The Art of Good Shooting – J. E. M. Ruffer
Archery for All – Daniel Roberts
Rowing for Everyone – Christopher Chant
Sea Fishing for Fun – Alan Wrangles and Jack P. Tupper

Holidays

Pony Trekking – Edward Hart
Inland Waterways – Charles Hadfield

Here is everything the beginner needs to know about an absorbing, very satisfying and highly economical leisure activity. The emphasis throughout is on the simplicity with which consistently drinkable wines and beers can be produced, with the minimum of equipment and time.

Contents

1 Water into Wine

Wine is one of the oldest drinks known to man; its origins go back to at least 2000 BC. It is, by dictionary definition, the fermented juice of the grape, but you can make wine from all sorts of other fruits, vegetables, grains, and even flowers and leaves.

It used to be the custom for practically everyone living in the country to make wines, usually from root vegetables such as parsnips, carrots and potatoes, and these wines were often very powerful indeed. Home wine making began to decline towards the end of the last century, when, because Great Britain was a prosperous country it was possible to buy imported wines very cheaply and it was simply not worth the time and trouble to make your own. The practice continued, though, in many country districts. It was not long, however, before the price of imported wines began to rise, and the government of the day saw a ready-made source of revenue and began to impose taxes on wines and spirits. The result of this was that home wine making began to gather momentum again and continued to do so up until the end of World War II. After a further period of little activity, interest in home wine making was aroused again and has reached almost epidemic proportions during the last ten to fifteen years.

A major contributing factor to this new interest is almost certainly the soaring prices of imported wine, despite promises made that cheap wine would be one of the benefits we could expect when Britain joined the EEC.

Why Make Wine?

This cost factor is probably the biggest single reason for making wine at home. Even if you just stick to making wines from concentrated grape juice – the easiest but most expensive way – your wine will cost you less than a sixth of the price of a comparable commercial wine. If you make it in fairly large quantities you can cut the cost to an eighth or even a tenth of the price of commercial wine. And if you make your wine from fresh fruits and berries, you can cut the cost to just the price of the sugar. At present-day

Very pleasant wines can be made from a wide variety of basic ingredients

values, this could be something like 4p a bottle if you use berries you have picked from the hedgerows.

But cost is only one aspect and there are many others. Most important of these is that drinking home made wine is a very pleasurable experience. You can make wines of all types from very dry table wines to heavy, sweet dessert wines and by the careful addition of herbs you can make very palatable vermouths. All of which means that you can enjoy your home made wine on its own or with a meal and you can drink different wines throughout a meal. All at very low cost.

Then you can use your wine in cooking. You can marinate cheap cuts of meat in home made wine to tenderize the meat and improve the flavour, you can add wine to casserole dishes, and you can use it in sweets and desserts.

Last, but certainly not least, you can get an awful lot of pleasure simply through making your wine. Home wine making is a hobby which you can easily tailor to the amount of time you have available. If, for example, you have only an hour or two a week to spare, you can make wines from canned concentrates, but if you want to make a major hobby out of it you can easily spend a few hours every evening in your winery making new batches, bottling, blending . . . and sampling!

Fermentation

When you taste a really good wine, it is difficult to think of it in terms of a biochemical reaction, yet that is exactly what it is. Yeast – which is a living organism – reacts with sugar in solution and converts it to ethyl alcohol, carbon dioxide gas, and heat energy. This reaction continues until all the sugar has been converted or until the alcoholic content of the solution (or 'must' as it is properly called) overcomes the yeast and kills it. The idea is to ferment the wine until it produces enough alcohol for the type of wine you want to make but not enough to kill the yeast.

The biochemical reaction I have just described therefore dictates, up to a point, what is needed to produce a wine. First you need some form of yeast, then you need some form of sugar in solution. Commercial wines are produced from grapes which are simply crushed to extract the juice and this forms the sugar solution. Natural yeasts on the skins of the grapes are then allowed to act on the solution and the result is a high quality wine. Grapes are about the only fruit from which you can make wine in this way and modern practice is to add a yeast culture to the grape pulp.

For your home made wines you need to make a sugar solution by using fruit, vegetables or flowers to provide flavour, colour and aroma, adding sugar and water to make up the volume and strength of the solution. Then you need to add yeast, and the best form is a proper wine yeast. Other ingredients are often necessary if you want to produce the best possible results – acid, vitamins, yeast nutrient, and so on – but I shall deal with these later.

Fermentation will only take place properly if the sugar solution is of the correct strength or specific gravity and if the solution is kept at the temperature at which the yeast is active. You can easily make sure that these conditions are met by measuring the specific gravity of the solution with a hydrometer and the temperature with a thermometer.

When you mix together all the ingredients for your wine, fermentation will start usually within twenty-four hours and will be quite violent at first. But it will die down to a gentle action after two or three days and will continue to work quietly until all the sugar has been converted to alcohol. This may take anything up to three or four months, or even longer, but do not be impatient; allow it to ferment to completion or you may end up with a weak, sweet wine.

Clarification

After fermentation is complete, it is best to add a Campden tablet to the wine and allow it to settle (these tablets are fully described later in this chapter). The wine will slowly begin to clear, all debris left over from fermentation gradually sinking to the bottom of the vessel. Siphon the wine, when clear, into a clean jar, add another Campden tablet and leave it to mature for 2–3 months. This is the part that will really test your patience.

If you have used a wine yeast culture you should find that the wine clears to a rich brilliance quite quickly. When it is clear, transfer the wine to another clean jar and leave it for a further three months to finish maturing.

Bottling

At the end of the six months' clearing and maturing time your wine will be ready to bottle, and this is where you have an opportunity to taste it. The best way to bottle wine is to siphon it from the storage jar into the bottles (and to siphon it you have to suck it through a tube!).

The way you bottle your wine is most important; if you do it properly, using wine bottles rather than old lemonade bottles, and finishing the job off with foil caps and labels, it shows some pride in your workmanship, and when you come to serve your wine to your friends, it gives a proper first impression of the wine and encourages your guests to treat it with the respect it deserves. I shall have a lot more to say about bottling later in the book.

Maturing

It is a well-known fact that wine does not keep — because once it is bottled the desire to drink it is almost overwhelming! But resist the temptation and you will be glad you did. If you allow your wine to mature in the bottles for preferably at least six months you will be rewarded by a much smoother, rounder and generally more palatable drink.

Store your bottles of wine on their sides in wine racks or bins so that the corks are kept constantly wet by the wine. The reason for this is that if the cork becomes dry it may allow air to enter through is pores, possibly bringing with it bacteria which could ruin your wine.

The Importance of Cleanliness

It is probably true to say that more home made wines are spoiled by carelessness over making sure that everything is perfectly clean than by any other single cause. By perfectly clean, I mean sterile.

The bacteria which can harm wine are hardy little fellows, so as a matter of course sterilize your equipment — including bottles and corks — before you use it. Fortunately, sterilizing your wine making equipment is a very simple task; all you need is a 10 per cent solution of sodium metabisulphite (which you can buy from any wine making supplier or most chemists). To make this solution, dissolve about two ounces of the sodium metabisulphite powder in a pint of water; the exact quantity of powder is not critical. Pour the solution into fermentation vessels, give it a good swill round and pour it out again. Soak the cork or bung for your fermentation vessel in the solution before use and use the solution in the fermentation lock which you fit to the vessel. Draw the solution through your siphon tube before you bottle your wine, but do not suck too hard because the solution tastes foul. Rinse your bottles with the solution and soak the corks in it. In fact, when in doubt give everything a rinse in the sterilizing solution.

Sterilizing the Wine

Not only is it important to sterilize all the equipment you use, but you must also keep the wine sterile at all stages of its production to kill off any bacteria which would spoil the wine.

One of the most effective sterilizing agents is sulphur fumes, and early wine makers, both commercial and private, used to burn sulphur in their fermentation vessels to sterilize them. Fortunately, modern science has provided us with a much simpler way of doing this by using a solution of sodium metabisulphite.

When you dissolve sodium metabisulphite in water it gives off sulphur dioxide and it is this gas which does the job of sterilizing the wine making equipment. Sodium metabisulphite is also available in the form of small tablets called Campden tablets which contain a given amount (0·44g or 7 grains) of the salt. It is in the form of these Campden tablets that sodium metabisulphite is easily added to the basic fruit or vegetable solution while fermentation is in progress. The gas given off by the Campden tablet fortunately evaporates very quickly and after a day or so there is no trace of the tell-tale sulphur dioxide smell. During this time the wine has been thoroughly sterilized.

Generally speaking, it is sufficient to add just one Campden tablet to each gallon of must at the fermentation stage. You may wonder why, if the sulphur dioxide gas will kill off bacteria and wild yeast growths present in your basic fruit or vegetable pulp, it will not kill off with equal efficiency the yeast which you add to the pulp in order for fermentation to take place. The answer to this lies in the fact that wine yeasts have been cultivated over a period of years with a built-in resistance to the sulphur dioxide while bacteria and wild yeasts have not. This means that when you mix your pulp or fruit juice solution and add the Campden tablet to sterilize it and wine yeast to start the fermentation, the action of this wine yeast, while it may be slowed by the sulphur dioxide, continues unabated after the gas has evaporated in two days or so.

Many amateur wine makers — including myself — have found that it is an advantage to add a Campden tablet to the wine when you siphon it (or rack it as it is more commonly known) off the debris left after fermentation is complete. In fact each subsequent time you transfer the wine from one jar to a clean one. The purpose of this is to kill any bacteria which may be picked up during the racking to prevent them from spoiling the wine. It has also been said by many experts that the use of Campden tablets at these stages helps to make the wine smoother, give it a better colour and better clarity. It will also prevent any further fermentation because the yeast has become virtually exhausted and is having to work extremely hard to keep its head above water, as it were, in the by now strongly alcoholic solution. Any further fermentation after the wine has been racked is undesirable especially, of course, if you have bottled the wine when it could cause the corks to blow and your precious wine would be lost.

I personally believe that the introduction of sodium metabisulphite — either in powder form or as Campden tablets — has had a profound effect on amateur wine making. As I have just explained, its use is extremely simple yet it can completely remove any chance of spoiled wine as a result of airborne bacteria and wild yeast growths. As a general rule, never never attempt to make a wine without sterilizing both your equipment and the must with the correct amount of sodium metabisulphite or Campden tablets.

Specific Gravity — the Wine Maker's Yardstick

Specific gravity can tell you more about your wine and its progress than any other single piece of equipment. If you know the specific gravity of your must when you first mix it before fermentation and the specific gravity at the end of fermentation you can, by looking up the table in Appendix 1, find out accurately how much alcohol your wine contains. And a step further on from this is that specific gravity readings allow you to design a wine of particular strength, sweetness or dryness.

But first, what is specific gravity?

Specific gravity is simply a measure of the weight of a liquid. For example, a thick, heavy liquid like treacle has a high specific gravity while a thin liquid like water has a low specific gravity. In fact water is taken as the standard of weight against which all other liquids are measured; it is said to have a specific gravity of 1.000.

The instrument used to measure specific gravity is called a hydrometer and I shall be dealing with the choice and use of the hydrometer in the next chapter.

2 What You Need and Where to Get It

The equipment you need in order to start making your own wines is very simple, inexpensive, and easy to obtain. To begin with all you need are a fermentation jar, an air lock, a siphon tube, and some bottles in which to store your wine. In addition to this basic list I would add a hydrometer and jar because I firmly believe that you cannot begin too early to use this instrument in your wine making.

If you follow my advice you will be starting your wine making by using a can of concentrated grape juice such as that available from most branches of Boots. The only ingredients you need in addition to this can of juice are sugar and yeast. Plus, of course, some Campden tablets or sodium metabisulphite with which to sterilize your equipment and wine.

Fermentation Vessels

The most popular type of fermentation vessel for home wine making is the one gallon glass demijohn which has become almost the traditional piece of equipment used by home wine makers. But in recent years plastic vessels have appeared on the market which are considerably cheaper and just as good. These are usually made from hard PVC, although I have seen some in soft PVC which are used inside a cardboard carton and can be folded flat when not in use.

Unfortunately, glass fermentation jars have recently become rather expensive but if you have a friendly off-licence or café nearby you can often buy suitable soft drinks jars quite cheaply. Plastic vessels, on the other hand, have become cheaper and have the advantage of being virtually unbreakable.

When you progress to making larger quantities of wine you will be able to buy special bucket-like containers in which five gallons or even more can be fermented at one time. These are invariably made of plastic and have a lid with provision in the centre for fitting a fermentation air lock. The large water carriers used by

The basic equipment you need for wine making. *Back* (*l to r*): one gallon demijohn for fermenting; airlock and cork; wine bottles; hydrometer and jar. *Front*: corking gun; siphon tube; corks; foil capsules; labels

campers and caravanners are also suitable for making large quantities of wine. They are often fitted with a tap at the bottom which can be useful when you come to rack the wine off the sediment after fermentation, the level of the tap generally being slightly higher than any debris left in the wine. If you intend to use one of these water carriers you will have to modify it slightly to allow a fermentation lock to be fitted, but this is a simple matter of cutting a hole in the top suitable for taking the air lock direct or fitted into its cork or rubber bung.

Fermentation Locks

In the early days of home wine making the failure rate could be fairly high because the wine was usually fermented in an open vessel covered only with a piece of muslin and airborne bacteria could get into it and completely ruin the brew. Possibly the biggest single advance in home wine making has been the introduction of the fermentation lock or air lock which has now been in constant use for several years. This device enables the carbon dioxide gas produced during fermentation to escape without allowing bacteria to enter the vessel.

Fermentation locks are available in several different types made of either glass or plastic, but they all work on the same basic principle. That principle is one of forcing the carbon dioxide gas to bubble out to the atmosphere through a water trap which obviously prevents bacteria entering the fermentation vessel. In this way it provides what is, in effect, a one-way valve.

You can use a plug of cotton wool in the neck of the fermentation jar instead of a proper air lock but locks are so cheap that it is not really worthwhile doing so because you stand the chance of ruining a gallon or more of perfectly good wine for the sake of a few pence spent on a proper fermentation lock.

In addition to keeping unwanted bacteria out of your wine, the fermentation lock provides a valuable instant check on whether the fermentation is still in progress or if, in fact, it has finished.

The most popular type of fermentation lock is a U-shaped tube with two bubbles in it, one in each arm of the U. You put water or sterilizing solution into the lock so that the level of this solution is roughly halfway up the bubble in each arm. When the level of the

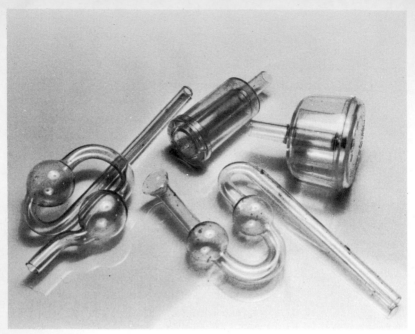

A variety of different fermentation locks. All work efficiently

solution is the same in each arm, fermentation has stopped, but if the level of solution in the outlet arm is higher than that in the inlet arm, fermentation is still in progress, even though you may not be able to see gas actually bubbling through the solution.

It is worth while putting a small plug of cotton wool in the outlet opening of the fermentation lock to prevent bits of dust and other foreign matter falling into the water or sulphite solution.

Siphon Tube

Since it is virtually impossible to pour wine from one large container to another without disturbing the sediment or 'lees', you should always use a siphon tube to do this job. It also prevents you spilling wine because pouring such large quantities from one vessel to another is a rather heavy job.

The best material for a siphon tube is quarter-inch bore polythene tubing which is available from all wine making suppliers and many chemists. It is better than rubber tubing because it does not tend to kink as rubber tubing does, and this can slow down or even stop the flow of wine from one container to the other.

Always attach a U-shaped tube to the end of the siphon tube which is in the demijohn of wine. The purpose of this is to prevent, as far as possible, the lees being drawn into the siphon tube and hence into the fresh container. By using the U-shaped tube, the wine is drawn downwards rather than up as a straight tube would do. Some siphon tubes which are available on the market have some form of tap fitted to the outlet end. While this is of great use during bottling wines because it allows you to cut off the flow of wine very easily, it is by no means essential; you can do the job very nearly as well by simply pinching the end of the tube.

Bottles and Corks

Nothing looks worse than serving a home made wine, no matter how good, from a bottle which was not properly designed to contain wine. Yet a great many amateur wine makers do so. But wine bottles are very easy to get hold of. Presumably, as a wine maker, you also drink commercial wines – at least until you reach the stage where the production of your home brew is sufficient to keep you going throughout the year. So you can simply save the bottles in which you bought your commercial wine. Then there are hotels; they throw out literally hundreds of wine bottles every week and if you have a quiet word with the manager of a local hotel, I feel sure that he will be only too glad to let you help yourself to as many empty wine bottles as you want. As a last resort, you can even buy them.

Proper wine corks are available from wine making suppliers and it is advisable always to use these. Never use corks which have already been used for something else; they may contain bacteria which will cause your wine to go off or, more importantly, they will retain a flavour from the previous wine which may impart itself into your own wine.

You will need a corker in order to insert normal straight sided wine bottle corks into your bottles with some degree of ease and these are available relatively cheaply from wine making suppliers.

To finish the job off you will need some labels and foil capsules to put over the corks and necks of the bottles.

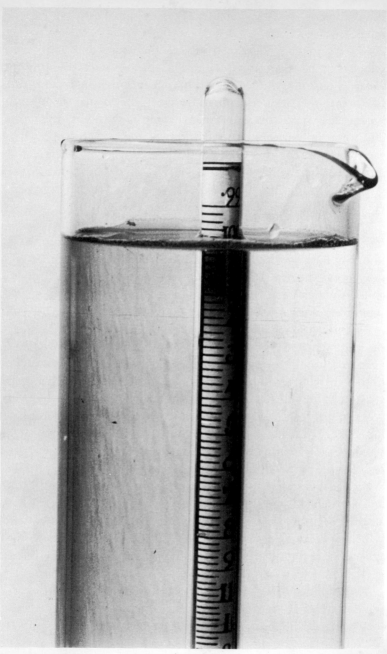

To read a hydrometer it is important to have your eye on the same level as the liquid

Hydrometer

I have purposely left the hydrometer to last in the list of equipment which you need for wine making because there is far more to say about it than about any of the other equipment.

As I pointed out in the last chapter, I consider the hydrometer to be an indispensable part of any wine maker's equipment because you can use it to tell you so many different things. For example, not only will the hydrometer tell you the specific gravity and hence potential alcohol content of your freshly mixed must, and the specific gravity of the wine when fermentation has finished, it will also give you an instant check on whether a fermentation has stuck (stopped for some reason before the full amount of potential alcohol has been produced).

A hydrometer consists of a glass tube weighted at the bottom so that when you place it in a liquid it floats upright. And the thinner the liquid the lower the hydrometer floats. The top part of the tube is calibrated with markings of specific gravity – usually from 0·990 to 1·150 or thereabouts – so by simply floating the instrument in a container of a liquid you can read the specific gravity of the liquid direct.

The way you read the hydrometer is quite important; you must have your eye on the same line as the level of the liquid. If it is higher or lower than the liquid level you will get a false reading. To take a reading it is best to pour a small quantity of must or wine into a special test cylinder of glass or clear plastic – sterilizing it first, of course – and lower the hydrometer gently into the liquid, making sure that it does not stick to the inside of the cylinder. When the hydrometer has stopped bobbing up and down, carefully take your reading.

Since the specific gravity of a liquid changes with temperature it is quite important to take all your readings at the same temperature; 15°C (60°F) is the figure usually recommended. So immediately before you make a specific gravity reading check the temperature of the must or wine and if it differs from 15°C adjust it. You can do this quite simply by standing the test cylinder containing the solution in a bowl of either hot or cold water until the temperature stabilizes at the correct level.

You can, however, use the hydrometer at other temperatures if you apply a correction factor to the reading. The chart opposite gives the corrections for temperatures between 10 and 30°C.

How the hydrometer can help you

If you fill a test cylinder with water at 15°C and place the hydrometer in it, you will find that the specific gravity indicated is 1·000. Now if you add sugar to the water, stirring until it is all dissolved, then take another hydrometer reading the specific gravity reading will have increased. This is because, by adding the sugar, you have made the solution heavier – and the hydrometer floats higher. The more sugar you add the heavier the solution becomes and the higher the specific gravity becomes.

The finished wine should have a specific gravity somewhere between 0·990 and 1·020 depending on the dryness or sweetness. Dry wines should be in the range 0·990 to 1·000, medium wines from 1·000 to 1·010, and sweet wines from 1·010 to 1·020. So the first thing your hydrometer allows you to do is adjust the sweetness of your wine to suit your own taste. You can ferment the must to complete dryness (S.G. 0·990) then add sugar a little at a time until the specific gravity reaches the figure you want.

But a much more important use of the hydrometer is in the design, as it were, of wines to a particular strength as well as sweetness. The potential alcohol content of a wine is proportional to the amount of sugar contained in the must before fermentation starts, so if you measure the specific gravity of the must you can find out, by looking at the table in Appendix 1 at the end of this book, what alcoholic content your wine will have. And what is more, if the wine will be too strong or not strong enough you can do something about it.

For instance, if the hydrometer reading shows that the potential alcohol content will be too low, you can add sugar to the must until the specific gravity reaches the figure which will give you the amount of alcohol you want. Here is an example.

Imagine you are making a fairly strong table wine from concentrated red grape juice and you want an alcohol content of about 14 per cent. The table in Appendix 1 shows that for this alcohol content the specific gravity of the must should be 1·105. However, when you measure the specific gravity with your hydrometer, it is

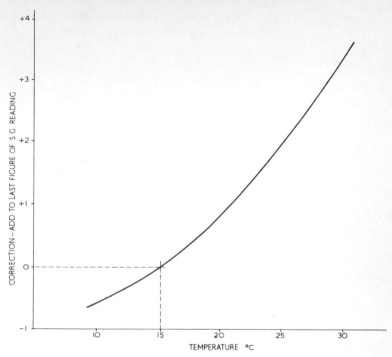

This chart enables you to correct a hydrometer reading, taken at any temperature, to what it would have been at 15°C. Simply measure the temperature, find the appropriate correction from the chart and add or subtract it from the last figure of the reading

only 1·080 which, according to the table, will only give an alcohol content of 10·6 per cent. Now if you look again at the table, you will see that to produce an alcohol content of 14 per cent there needs to be 2lb 12oz of sugar in a gallon of the must. But to produce 10·6 per cent alcohol there is only 2lb 1oz of sugar. So to make your must capable of producing the required 14 per cent alcohol you simply add 11oz of sugar to the mixture and check the specific gravity again.

On the other hand, if the initial specific gravity is too high you simply add water to the must to reduce it to the figure which will give you the strength of wine you want. As a guide, table wines usually have an alcohol content of between 9 per cent for lightish wines to 14 per cent for stronger ones, while dessert wines can go up to 17 or 18 per cent.

So you can see just how useful your hydrometer can be; it can take all the guesswork out of winemaking. But do not become a slave to it. You do not need to know the alcohol content of your wine to a tenth of 1 per cent — an approximate indication is perfectly adequate.

Sacrometer

An instrument which has appeared on the market comparatively recently and which looks almost identical to a hydrometer is the sacrometer. In fact it works in exactly the same way as a hydrometer but it has a simplified scale calibrated from 0 to 55 which bears no relationship to actual specific gravity readings. The scale also contains several coloured bands. At the top there are yellow, red and blue bands which indicate dry, medium and sweet finished wines respectively, while at the bottom there is a rather broader green band which indicates the starting specific gravity range for table wines.

If you prefer a simplified instrument such as this rather than measuring actual specific gravities and converting them for the information you want, a sacrometer will serve you just as well as a hydrometer will.

Ingredients

The basic ingredient of any home made wine is the fruit, vegetable, or concentrate that you use. However, I do not propose to deal with this basic ingredient here because I shall be doing so in detail in the next two chapters.

Yeast

There are many different kinds of yeast available and many of the recipes for home made wines and beers which you find in old cookery books call for baker's yeast to be used. But this was general because at the time these books were written baker's yeast was the only type freely available.

It is possible to make quite respectable wines and beers with baker's yeast, but it can cause one or two rather difficult problems. The most important of these is that when fermentation has finished baker's yeast will not settle to the bottom of the wine or beer in a compact layer as proper wine and beer yeasts will and tends to get stirred up when you try to siphon the wine or beer off the sediment at the bottom of the vessel.

Another problem is that the use of baker's yeast may give off-flavours to the wine or beer, especially if you leave the brew on the lees for any length of time after fermentation has finished. On the whole it is much better to use a proper wine or beer yeast for your home made drinks. These special yeasts are not expensive, they are readily available and you can use them to impart a particular character to your wines and beers.

Wine yeasts are available in a wide variety of different types and can be bought as liquids, powders or tablets. You can now buy cultures of wine yeasts covering all the popular types of wine – hock, burgundy, claret, port, riesling, sherry and so on – which will impart their own characteristic to the wine you make, especially if you are making wine from concentrated grape juice. You can, for example, produce two quite different wines from the same type of grape juice simply by using different yeasts.

Many of the special wine yeasts now available – especially those in tablet form – incorporate some form of nutrient to help them to ferment properly.

In addition to yeasts which are cultivated from specific wine types, most companies also produce what they call an all-purpose wine yeast. This is a yeast which will produce a quite drinkable and acceptable wine without having a particular distinctive characteristic.

When you start your wine off, whatever type of yeast you are using, you can simply add it direct to the gallon of must, but this I find tends to make the fermentation rather slow to start. I find that I get better results – as well as a faster start to the fermentation – by mixing the yeast in a starter bottle together with a good yeast nutrient. When this is fermenting thoroughly I add it to the must in the fermentation vessel and this gives a quick start and thorough fermentation to the must.

Using a starter bottle

When you buy your wine yeast it is in a state of suspended animation, as it were, and before it can start to work on the must it has to be reactivated. The best way to do this is in a starter bottle.

The ideal vessel for a starter bottle is one of the half-pint non-returnable glass bottles which 'Sch . . . you know who' use for their mixers. Sterilize the bottle and into it pour a tablespoon of concentrated grape juice or half an ounce of chopped raisins, a teaspoon of sugar, a good squeeze of lemon juice, some vitaminized yeast nutrient (the correct amount will depend on the particular make you buy and will be given on its packet) and the yeast culture either in liquid, powder or tablet form. In the case of tablet yeasts I find it better to crush the tablet between two spoons before adding it to the starter bottle. Make up the quantity in the starter bottle to a quarter of a pint using water which has been boiled and allowed to cool to lukewarm. Give the bottle a good shake to mix all the ingredients together then plug the neck with a wad of plain cotton wool (not the medicated type).

Stand your starter bottle in a warm place such as an airing cupboard and leave it for twenty-four hours. At the end of this time it should be bubbling quite well and be ready for you to add to the must in the fermentation jar.

Beer Yeasts

In the same way that you can buy a variety of different wine yeasts, there are several yeasts available now which are specially made for brewing beer and will give characteristic mild, bitter, lager, etc, flavours. In general these yeasts are rather more active than wine yeasts and I have never found it necessary to use a starter bottle; I just throw the yeast in with the rest of the mixture and let it get on with fermentation.

All beer yeasts with the exception of that used for brewing lager are what is known as top-fermenting types. That is to say they work at the top of the solution or 'wort' and eventually form a thick layer covering the whole of the top of the wort. Lager yeasts, on the other hand, are bottom-fermenters and, as the name implies, they settle at the bottom of the wort in the same way as a wine yeast and although it may appear to be working much more slowly than the more usual top-fermenters, it does its job just as well and produces beer of equal quality. In fact, I have used a lager type yeast for all sorts of different beers and find that it produces

Always activate the yeast in a starter bottle to ensure thorough fermentation

excellent results in a wide variety of different worts.

Although a starter bottle is not necessary for beer yeasts, you can if you prefer use one, but in this case replace the grape juice or chopped raisins with a tablespoon of malt extract.

Sugars

Sugar is one of the fundamental ingredients necessary to wine making and there are all kinds of different sugars available. Many home wine makers insist on using special sugars such as invert sugar, glucose, and so on, but I have always found that I get perfectly satisfactory results using plain simple granulated household sugar.

Granulated sugar is a highly refined and purified form of sugar which has the advantages of being easily available and very cheap. It also has the very important advantage of not changing the characteristic flavour or colour of the wine as some other sugars do.

In short, I suggest that you use granulated sugar for all your home wine making. There is just one exception, though. Brown sugar such as Demerara or Barbados sugar can add a little something to the flavour of richer wines like sherry, but you may find that you need a slightly different amount from the quantity of sugar given in the recipe which (at least in this book) is always given for white sugar. So the safest way is to add as much sugar as is necessary to bring the specific gravity of the must up to the level you need for the type of wine you want to make.

The method of adding sugar to the must is quite important. Never simply tip it into the must in the fermentation vessel because it will simply sink to the bottom and form a hard layer which will not dissolve. Instead, dissolve the sugar in a small quantity of warm water or must to form a syrup then add this to the rest of the must. This way you can make sure that the sugar is completely dissolved before you pour it into the fermentation vessel.

Additives

The most important additive to the must, apart from yeast nutrient, is an acid. Citric acid is the most widely used. It is present naturally in oranges, lemons and other citric fruits, of course, and recipes which contain these fruits should need no further addition of the acid. But all other recipes should have citric acid added and the crystalline form available from chemists and wine making suppliers is by far the most convenient and satisfactory method of adding it.

The purpose of the acid is to ensure rapid and thorough fermentation and it is usually used at the rate of about two teaspoons to a gallon of must. Another very useful acid in wine making is lactic acid which you can add to the must at the rate of one teaspoon per gallon. This acid helps the wine to form a much better aroma and a rounder, smoother taste after it has matured for a year or so.

A yeast nutrient helps the must to ferment better and more thoroughly to convert all the sugar contained in it into alcohol and carbon dioxide. There are several proprietary nutrients on the market, mostly in tablet form, and no particular one seems to me to be better than any other. So you are fairly safe in using whichever one your local wine supplier has in stock. But do, please, use yeast nutrient; it is as vital to the successful making of wine as yeast itself.

Tannin is vital to the good keeping properties of wine. It is present in a natural state on the skins of most fruits, but in many cases a recipe will call for a small amount of strong cold tea – usually about a tablespoon to a gallon – to be added to the must to get sufficient tannin into the wine. A secondary benefit of tannin is that it gives a hint of bitterness to the wine which can accentuate the flavour of the wine.

A pectic enzyme, which is usually known by its shortened name of pectozyme, is valuable in extracting flavour and colour from fruits. The juice of the fruit is contained within cells which need to be broken down if you are to get the maximum flavour and colour from the fruit. When you prepare your fruit for wine making you must crush it to break down the fruit as much as possible, but obviously you cannot possibly hope to break down every cell. If you add a teaspoon of pectozyme to the fruit pulp it will continue the work of breaking down the cells containing the juice and prevent microscopic unbroken cells remaining in the wine which would cause it to become cloudy when fermentation is finished. So

Wine making additives (*l to r*): tannin; sodium metabisulphite; yeast nutrient; pectic enzyme; cirtic acid

always use pectozyme in wines which you make from fruit, berries and vegetables to ensure a clear, bright finished wine.

Pectic enzyme has a secondary use, too. If you have produced a wine which refuses to clear, it is almost certainly due to pectin haze as a result of the cellular structure of the fruit not being properly broken down. So you can add pectozyme to the finished wine and in most cases this will clear the wine. I shall have more to say about this in later chapters.

Where to Buy your Equipment

These days there are very few major towns at least which do not have a wine making supplier which specializes in equipment and ingredients for home wine makers. But even if the place where you live does not boast such a supplier, there is usually a chemist nearby who has expanded into the wine making side. For example, several branches of Boots now sell the necessary equipment and ingredients.

Another means of buying your supplies is by mail order. There are several companies throughout the country which specialize in this and I have included a list of some of them at the end of the book.

The equipment dealt with in this chapter is all that you need to make a start in wine making. Later on you may want to add other items, but you will probably do so as and when you need this extra equipment. But one additional piece which you may find useful if you do not have a convenient airing cupboard in which to put your fermenting must is a thermostatically controlled heater. This is rather like an aquarium heater and thermostat combined which you place in the demijohn containing the must. It automatically keeps the must at the correct temperature for thorough fermentation and uses very little electricity in doing so.

Many companies now supply complete kits for beginners containing everything you need to make a start in wine making. It is worthwhile considering buying one of these kits, which also usually include a can of concentrated grapejuice for you to make your first gallon.

3   Starting Simply

I firmly believe that it is important psychologically to have success at your first attempt at wine making. In the first place it gives you much-needed encouragement and secondly it shows you just how easy wine making really is. For this reason, I suggest that you make your first gallon of home made wine using concentrated grape juice, fruit juice or fruit pulp as the base.

Let us look first of all at concentrated grape juice. There is a wide variety of different types of concentrated grape juice available today and most are very good indeed. These commercial grape juices are blends of juices from several different wine-growing regions of Europe which have been concentrated by a vacuum process and then canned or bottled. The secret of a good concentrate lies in the blending to adjust the final flavour of the juice so that it meets the demands of home wine makers in this country.

When the juice has been concentrated it contains a fairly high proportion of sugar which is, of course, natural grape sugar and in some cases at least, you do not need to add any further sugar to the must in order to produce the wine satisfactorily. In other cases you need to add a certain amount of sugar, but only rarely is this more than about a pound.

The price of concentrated grape juice varies from about £1 to £2 for sufficient to make one gallon. The lower price concentrates are those to which you must add further sugar and the higher price ones are those to which no addition is necessary.

A fairly new innovation in concentrated grape juices are those which are supplied as part of a complete kit with which, it is claimed, you can make a wine ready to drink in three weeks. I shall have more to say about these new products a little later in the chapter. But first, I shall describe how to make a gallon of wine with a normal concentrated grape juice.

Making Wine with Grape Juice Concentrates

For your first gallon of wine I recommend you to buy a can of grape juice from one of the well known home wine making

Typical packed ingredients for wine making, together with a selection of wine yeasts

manufacturers such as Boots, Southern Vineyard, CWE, Unican, and so on.

Once you have bought the concentrate, the first thing to do is read the instructions thoroughly. In this chapter I am dealing with a specific make of grape juice and the instructions with other products may vary slightly, so treat this chapter as being written in general terms and check the instructions with your own particular can of juice in case you need to do something different.

First of all you will need to mix up a starter bottle with the yeast you are going to use for your gallon of wine following the instructions given in the previous chapter. For this first attempt, incidentally, choose a general purpose yeast; you can graduate to specific wine types a bit later when you have had some experience. Make up the starter bottle preferably the day before you intend to start making your wine.

On the great day you must begin operations by sterilizing all equipment using the sodium metabisulphite solution or Campden tablets. Wash the fermentation jar and other pieces of equipment well then give them a good rinse round with the sterilizing solution and tip it away. Do not rinse the items again once you have sterilized them.

Pour the contents of the can of grape juice concentrate into the fermentation vessel allowing plenty of time for all the juice to drain out of the can. Add six pints of tepid water at about 77°F (25°C) using some of the water to rinse out the concentrate can to ensure that all the juice is removed. Mix the water and juice together until they are completely uniform.

Add the starter bottle contents to the fermentation jar, making sure all the yeast is removed from the bottle and shake the demijohn to ensure that everything is mixed together well. Seal the fermentation vessel with an airlock and place the jar in the bottom of an airing cupboard or other warm place. Leave it to ferment for about ten days, giving it a shake every morning to help promote thorough fermentation. At the end of this time, take a specific gravity reading; the specific gravity should be about 1·010. If it is higher than this leave the wine to ferment for another two or three days and check the specific gravity again. When the specific gravity reaches 0·010 add five ounces of white sugar to a pint of the wine and stir thoroughly until it is completely dissolved. You will find it easier to dissolve the sugar if you warm the wine gently. (But do not allow it to become too hot or you may ruin the flavour of the wine.) Pour this pint of wine with its dissolved sugar back into the rest of the wine and replace the vessel in the airing cupboard. Allow it to ferment for another five days, shaking it gently each day, then check the specific gravity again. By this time it should have reached a level of 1·002. If it has not yet reached this figure, replace it and check the specific gravity each day until it has.

Add another five ounces of sugar to a pint of the wine, stirring until it is completely dissolved and return this to the fermentation jar. Now make up the total quantity of wine in the jar to one gallon with boiled water that you have allowed to cool to about 25°C (77°F). Return the fermentation jar to the airing cupboard again and allow it to ferment until it has completely finished. This will take about four weeks more and after this time check daily that there are still bubbles of gas passing through the fermentation lock. When these have stopped, the fermentation is complete.

The first stage in making wine from a concentrate, after sterilizing the fermentation vessel, is to pour in the concentrate

Add the required quantity of tepid water

Check the specific gravity of the wine, which should by now be 0·996. If it is higher than this the fermentation is still in progress although it is probably too slow for you to see the bubbles of gas passing through the fermentation lock. So return the fermentation vessel to the airing cupboard and leave it for another week, then check the specific gravity again. Continue to do this until the specific gravity of 0·996 is reached. It is necessary to do this so that the finished wine will have the correct amount of alcohol in it as well as having the correct balance of dryness.

Always remember that if a wine is too dry you can easily sweeten it by adding a little more sugar, but if it is too sweet, there is not very much you can do about it short of blending with a drier wine.

When fermentation has finished add a Campden tablet – crush it before you mix it with the wine – and leave the fermentation vessel in a cool place to allow the wine to clear with all the yeast and other debris settled at the bottom of the jar. When the wine is clear, siphon it off into a clean, sterilized gallon jar, taking care not to disturb any of the sediment left in the bottom of the fermentation vessel. Add a further crushed Campden tablet to help preserve the wine against the mild off-flavours which can form in newly-fermented wine.

Leave the wine in its storage jar for two to three months. If you are impatient to get your first gallon of wine clear so that you can bottle it and taste it, there is a short cut that you can take. It is called fining. Wine finings is a liquid which you mix with the wine and leave for about a week. During this time the liquid finings will settle to the bottom of the jar, taking with it all suspended particles of yeast and other debris, leaving a clear, bright wine which you can bottle straight away.

The important thing to remember when using liquid wine finings is that it must be evenly dispersed throughout the wine if it is going to work properly. The best method to ensure this is to pour the wine finings into a sterilized one pint bottle, then add the wine to the finings until the bottle is between half and three-quarters full. Screw a cap on the bottle and shake vigorously for about half a minute then pour the wine and finings back into the storage jar. Give the storage jar a vigorous shake as well so that the

Pour in the contents of the yeast starter bottle

Fit an air lock and identifying label

37

wine finings becomes evenly distributed throughout the entire gallon of wine.

When the wine is clear and has matured for two to three months — if you decide not to use the liquid wine finings — bottle the wine in clean, sterilized bottles and cork it. Now leave the wine for at least three months to mature in the bottles, preferably in a cool, dark place. Bottling is covered in detail in Chapter 7.

Before you bottle your wine, though, do a last check on the specific gravity with your hydrometer or sacrometer; you may even try some if you like! But bear in mind that it will taste a little raw at this stage. If the wine is too dry for your taste, as indicated by the hydrometer, this is the stage at which to sweeten it. But add the sugar only a little at a time — say half an ounce — making sure that each half ounce is thoroughly dissolved before you check the specific gravity again. Remember that medium wines should have a specific gravity up to $1 \cdot 010$ and sweet wines up to $1 \cdot 020$.

One thing it is well worthwhile doing when making your first gallon of wine (and any subsequent gallons if it comes to that) is to keep a notebook in which you can record the progress of your wine giving the date you started, the date you added the extra sugar, the final specific gravity, and the amount of sugar, if any, you added to adjust the taste of your wine, together with the specific gravity when you bottled it.

If you follow the instructions with your can of concentrated grape juice carefully, and I must repeat here that the instructions I have just given are for the Boots product and are by no means universal, you should produce an excellent wine at your first attempt. Many home wine makers go no further into the hobby than producing wines from concentrated grape juices. In fact there is quite a lot to be said for this because it takes very little time and with a small amount of effort you can make a wide variety of wine by buying the most suitable grape juice to make a particular type. You can make wines of different qualities by using grape juices of different qualities — from plain simple plonk up to really excellent wines that compare well with the best commercial products available. But whichever way you look at it, you can produce six bottles of very good wine for the same as it would cost you to buy just one bottle of commercial wine.

After twenty-four hours the wine should be fermenting well

Boots WINE-MAKING Winemakers Record Card

NAME OF WINE _HOCK_

Gallons _1_ **No.** _4/77_

Ingredients	Quantities
Hock concentrated grape juice (Boots)	_1 can_
Water	_To 1 gal total_
Sugar	_10 oz total_
Campden Tablets	_3 total_
Nutrient	
Tannin	_5 drops_
Acid	
Pectozyme	

Yeast Used _Unican Hock._

Date Yeast Added _4th March_ 19 _77_

Date Started _3rd March_ 19 _77_

Method _Dilute concentrate as directed_
Add yeast. Ferment down to S.G. 1·010
Add 5 oz sugar Ferment down to S.G. 1·002
Add 5 oz sugar Ferment to S.G. 0·996

Always note carefully the ingredients and procedure for each wine you make. This ensures repeatability

Three-week Wine

Over the last two or three years several kits have been on sale which claim to enable you to produce finished wine in only three weeks from start to finish. Typical of these products is the Unican kit which contains a can of grape juice concentrate, wine yeast, wine finings, and other additives. Everything you need, in fact, to make the wine. The concentrate is made from very high quality grape juice and no additional sugar is needed. (With some three-week wine kits the method varies and it is necessary to add sugar.)

The procedure for making these three-week wines is basically similar to the method I have just given for normal concentrated grape juice, but fermentation is complete in a much shorter time. The table given in the instructions for the Unican kit gives the fermentation time as being between six and sixteen days depending on the temperature where you stand the fermentation jar.

One difference between this and normal concentrate wines is that the manufacturers say that the specific gravity at the end of the fermentation should be between $1 \cdot 010$ and $1 \cdot 014$. But even though this is the range of medium wines, they say that wine produced to this specific gravity will taste dry.

When you siphon the wine off the yeast sediment into a clean jar, you must dissolve the contents of a small packet marked potassium sorbate in a little lukewarm water and add it to the wine. Potassium sorbate acts as a stabilizer and is a bacteria killing agent. The reason for adding it to the wine is to make sure that any yeast left in the wine after racking it off the sediment is killed and the wine is then stable. This eliminates any chance of a secondary fermentation starting after you have bottled the wine and forcing the corks out of the bottles.

After two days at room temperature you must siphon the wine into another clean storage jar and add liquid wine finings which is provided with the kit. In fact there are two sachets of wine finings, one which is clear and rather thick and the other which is a light straw colour. But the straw colour is very light indeed and you have to look very closely to tell the two apart. First of all add the contents of the sachet of colourless finings, shake the jar, then add the contents of the other sachet — the straw coloured finings — shake the jar again and leave at room temperature for two days. At the end of this time your wine should be clear and you can siphon it into yet another clean jar and leave it for another two days.

If the wine has not cleared after fining, there is another packet contained in the kit labelled Bentonite. Add this to a little of the wine, mixing thoroughly, and pour it into the storage jar, mix well, and leave it for two days before siphoning off once again. But it is important that you only use the Bentonite if the wine has refused to clear naturally.

After this stage you can bottle your wine and it is ready for you to drink, although like any wine it will improve with keeping.

In many ways it is a good idea to use one of these three-week wine kits for your first attempt because it does introduce you to the procedures of wine making fairly well and yet gives you a chance to sample the results of your efforts after a relatively short time. I have always found that by far the most difficult part of wine making is keeping enough patience to wait for the wine to mature properly to the state when it can be drunk with pleasure. These three-week kits buy you time by cutting out the waiting period and give you something to drink while you are making more conventional wines which do take rather longer. But of course, if you find that the three-week wines are to your taste, there is absolutely nothing to stop you making them all the time.

Other Concentrated Fruit Juices

There are several other fruit juices available in concentrated form, especially apple juice, which are suitable for making wine, and there are several fruit juices blended with grape concentrate to produce very pleasant and palatable wines.

The procedure for making wines with these juices is basically the same as for conventional concentrated grape juice, so I will not go through it all again here. In any case, full instructions are always included on the can or bottle.

Fruit Pulps

An alternative way of making wines simply and without a lot of time spent in preparing fruit, is to use a fruit pulp, of which there are a great many varieties available from home wine making suppliers. Again, I shall go through the procedure of making a

The contents of a typical three-week wine kit. Use one of these kits when you want good results fast

typical wine from a fruit pulp. In this case, orange wine made from Beach's Prepared Oranges for Winemaking.

This product makes a very pleasant dessert wine if you make it rather on the sweet side and an equally acceptable aperitif if you ferment it rather drier. The instruction leaflet on the can gives the amounts of sugar needed for the various types of wine. I have found that $3\frac{1}{4}$lb gives a very good dessert wine and $2\frac{1}{2}$lb if I am going to use the wine as an aperitif. But I must stress that these quantities are to suit my own particular taste and it is best for you to make up your own mind on the quantities of sugar when you have tried the wine.

As with making wine from grape juice concentrate, begin by making up a starter bottle with the yeast of your choice. I have found that a Tokay yeast is very good for producing a dessert wine while a Sherry yeast gives a good aperitif. But you will find that using an all-purpose yeast will give perfectly acceptable results in either case.

Tip the contents of the can of oranges into a saucepan and add approximately half a pint of water. Bring this mixture to the boil, stirring constantly to prevent any chance of the oranges burning. When the mixture has boiled allow it to cool and strain it into a fermentation jar, squeezing as much juice out of the pulp as possible. Add the sugar and a tablespoon of pectic enzyme together with the contents of the yeast starter bottle and make up to the full gallon with water. If you want to check the specific gravity at this point it should be about 1·130 for a dessert wine while for an aperitif it should be about 1·110. If it is a little higher than these figures it will not make a great deal of difference, it just means that the wine will be a little stronger or sweeter. But if it is lower I suggest that you add a little more sugar to bring it up to the required level. Fit a fermentation lock to the jar and stand it in a warm place to ferment to completion. This will take about six weeks.

When the fermentation is complete, add a crushed Campden tablet to the wine and allow it to settle before siphoning off into a clean storage jar. Add another Campden tablet and allow the wine to finish clearing before racking it off into wine bottles. Although the wine will be ready to drink in about eight weeks, let it stand to mature in the bottles as long as you are able to resist drinking it.

I have quoted this orange wine method, not because I think it is any better than other wines from fruit pulps, but because it is typical of the method, and I have made several really superb wines from cans of Beach's Prepared Oranges.

An interesting variation on wine made from fruit pulps is to mix together a can of fruit pulp and a can of concentrated grape juice to make two gallons of wine from the mixture. Again, using the orange pulp as an example, this method makes a very good full-bodied table wine if you use a yeast such as Graves or Chablis. In this case it is better to ferment the wine to approaching complete dryness. For this I suggest that you use about 3 pounds of sugar to the two gallons. This should give an initial specific gravity of about 1·090 to 1·095 which will produce an alcohol content in the finished wine of around 12 to $12\frac{1}{2}$ per cent.

The best way to produce this orange and grape juice wine is to begin fermentation in a bucket. Dissolve the sugar with hot water and pour it into the bucket, then add the fruit and grape juice and stir well. Make up to about 14 pints with cold water and add a teaspoon of citric acid, yeast nutrient, and the yeast solution from the starter bottle. Cover the bucket with a clean tea towel and leave to ferment for one to two days.

When the fermentation is well under way add two tablespoons of pectic enzyme. Leave the mixture to ferment for another five to seven days then strain it in equal quantities into two one gallon fermentation jars. Top the jars up to a gallon each with water which you have poured through the fruit pulp in the sieve. Fit fermentation locks to the two demijohns and place in a warm spot to complete fermentation. At the end of the fermentation period, rack the wine off the lees and clarify and bottle it in the usual way.

There is no doubt that concentrated grape and fruit juices and fruit pulp have been responsible to a large extent for the increase in popularity of home wine making because they make the whole procedure so very simple and foolproof. Which is why I suggest that you start your wine making activities in this way then, when you have had a few successes you may feel ready to move on to making your own wines from fresh and dried fruit, berries and vegetables.

4 Wine from Fresh Ingredients

While making wine from concentrated grape juices and fruit pulp gives you very drinkable wine with the minimum of fuss, there is no doubt that making your own wines from fruit you have prepared yourself – perhaps even picked yourself – gives you a much greater sense of achievement. You feel, quite rightly, that you have been involved right from the start. But it does, of course, involve rather more time and effort than making wine from concentrates. On the other hand, making wines from fresh ingredients can cut the cost of your wine making to minute proportions. For example you can use fruit which is left over from other activities such as jam making; you can use surplus vegetables from your garden; and you can even make wine from pea pods. If you live close to a fruit market or market garden you can often pick up fruit cheaply, especially if there is some left over late on a Saturday evening which would be unsuitable for sale by Monday.

Virtually all fruits and edible berries are suitable for wine making and those you choose are largely a matter of personal taste. But among the most popular are plums, apples, damsons, pears, blackberries, black currants, elderberries, gooseberries, and so on. Many vegetables also make superb wines, such as potatoes, parsnips, carrots, and marrows. You can make wine from flower petals such as elderflowers, roses, broom, and hawthorn blossom, although I must confess I have never been particularly fond of wines made from flowers. You can even make a very pleasant wine from cold tea or coffee, and the mead you can make from honey is quite exquisite.

Preparing the Fruit

Always use the best quality fruit you can get hold of; remember, the better the fruit, the better the wine.

Remove any badly bruised or rotten parts of the fruit with a knife and remove as many stalks and leaves as possible. Wash the fruit thoroughly to remove dust, chemical insecticides, wild yeasts,

The first stage – chopping the fruit

and the like. Immerse hard fruit such as apples and pears in water and scrub them with a soft scrubbing brush to remove as much dirt as possible. But with berries and other soft fruit this treatment would obviously damage them, so place them in a sieve or colander and rinse them thoroughly with cold running water. Chop large fruit roughly and remove pips and stones, or put hard fruit through a mincer.

Extracting the juice

There are several ways in which you can extract the juice from your prepared fruit, but the simplest, as far as the casual wine maker is concerned, is by fermenting on the pulp. It has the major advantage of not needing bulky and expensive equipment like a fruit press or steam extractor and produces, in my opinion, wine every bit as good as the other processes, if not better.

Place the fruit in a colourless polythene bucket (coloured ones have been known to have the colouring dye leached out during wine making) together with any additional base ingredients such as chopped raisins or grape juice concentrate if you are using them.

Ferment on the pulp in a covered bucket and keep in a warm place

Strain the liquid off the pulp, transfer to a demijohn and ferment under an airlock

Boil half the final quantity of water and pour it on the fruit (eg four pints if you are making a gallon of wine). Stir well, cover with a clean tea towel and leave to cool.

When the fruit is cool – at about 25°C (77°F) – crush a Campden tablet and stir it into the mixture. After twenty-four hours, crush the fruit with a wooden spoon or with your hands, and add about a third of the final quantity of sugar. You can, if you like, dissolve the sugar in a pint or two of warm water before adding it to make sure it is all dissolved.

Now stir in any additives you are going to use – citric acid, lactic acid, tannin (in the form of cold tea or tannin concentrate), and pectozyme – together with yeast nutrient and the contents of the yeast starter bottle (which you will have prepared the day before). Stir thoroughly, cover the bucket with a clean tea towel again, and stand it in a warm place for about three days. Stir the fruit well each day.

The small amount of alcohol formed during this early stage of fermentation helps to extract the flavour, colour, and aroma from the fruit in a much more efficient way than other extraction processes can, producing a much richer wine.

At the end of the three day fermentation on the pulp, strain the must through a sieve or straining bag into a fermentation jar. Press the pulp to extract the maximum amount of liquid but do not throw the pulp away. In most cases you can make another gallon of wine from it, especially with fruit like damsons and plums and berries such as blackberries, blackcurrants, and elderberries. Simply return the pulp to the bucket (after first washing and sterilizing the bucket) add a pound of chopped raisins or half a pint of concentrated grape juice, and repeat the whole procedure. I have found on one or two occasions that this second gallon is even better than the first!

Fermenting under Airlock

To the juice which you have strained into the fermentation vessel, add the other two-thirds of the total quantity of sugar, making sure it is all completely dissolved. Again you can dissolve the sugar in a pint of warmed must and add it to the jar in this way if you prefer. Top up the must to its final volume with boiled, cooled water and check the specific gravity, which will obviously depend on the particular wine you are making. If necessary, make any adjustments by adding a little more sugar or extra water.

Place the fermentation jar in the airing cupboard with a label tied to its neck to identify it. Leave it for about a month then rack off the lees into a clean, sterile jar and leave it to ferment out to completion, shaking gently each day. But first, top it up to its final quantity again with boiled, cooled water. And do not forget to transfer the tie-on label to the new bottle.

At the end of the fermentation period crush a Campden tablet and add it to the wine, mixing well, and leave the fermentation vessel in a cool place. This will allow the wine to clear with all the used yeast settling at the bottom of the jar.

When the wine has cleared siphon it off into a clean jar, leaving all the sediment at the bottom of the fermentation vessel. Add another crushed Campden tablet to help preserve the wine, and leave it in this storage jar for two to three months. As with making wine from concentrated grape juice, you can if you wish shorten this time by using liquid wine finings to clear the wine.

After the two to three month maturing period the wine should be clear and bright and it will then be ready for bottling. Check the specific gravity of the wine with your hydrometer and make any necessary final adjustments to the sweetness of the wine then siphon it into clean, sterile wine bottles and cork them.

Using Dried Fruits

During the winter, fresh fruit is often difficult to come by at a reasonable price – especially soft fruit –and a good alternative which will enable you to carry on making wine throughout the winter is to use dried fruits. You can buy dried apricots, dried peaches, dried apples, raisins, sultanas and many other fruits from wine making suppliers or from health food shops.

Dried fruit is also, in many ways, better for home wine making than fresh fruit because it tends to contain a higher proportion of sugar. Because fresh fruit contains a lot of water you need far less dried fruit; as a general rule, about a third of the amount of dried fruit to fresh fruit is ample.

There are two ways in which you can deal with dried fruit for wine making. The first is simply to chop it up, place it in a bucket and cover with boiling water, then leave to cool before adding the yeast and other ingredients in the same way as you do for fresh fruit. The second method is slightly more involved but does produce a better wine. First soak the dried fruit for eight to twelve hours in a large basin of water. Strain, chop or mince it, and put it into the fermenting bucket. Pour over half the final quantity of boiling water, allow to cool and proceed as for fresh fruit.

Of the dried fruits that are available, raisins and sultanas make admirable wine being the closest to a true wine made from grapes that you can get, especially if you use a proper wine yeast of the particular type for the wine you want to produce. Dried apricots, too, make a superb sweetish dessert wine if you ferment them with a Sauterne or Tokay yeast. In fact, one of the main advantages of making wines from dried fruit is that during fermentation the dried fruit tends to lose practically all of its own flavour and take on that of the yeast you are using instead, producing very much more 'winey' wines.

Dried fruits such as sultanas, raisins and apricots, make delicious wines

Wine from Flowers

Because flowers do not contain any of the substances on which yeast feeds to produce a really thorough fermentation, you have to add nutrients, acids, vitamins, and so on to the must. In fact the only things flowers will give to the wine are fragrance, colour and flavour. So you need to add chopped raisins or grape juice concentrate in order to give sufficient body to the wine. And to avoid the wine being dull and flat, you need to add quite a lot of tannin.

Picking and preparing the flowers

Make sure that the flowers are completely dry when you pick them – a warm sunny day is the best time – and do not leave them in the bag or basket you put them in for any longer than you have to otherwise they may become bruised. Remove all the stalks, leaves, and other green parts so that you are left with just the flower heads. This stripping of the green parts is vital because if left on they will give the wine a rather bitter flavour.

Wash the flower heads thoroughly to remove any dust and insecticides then sterilize them by rinsing in a gallon of water in which you have dissolved two crushed Campden tablets. Finally, rinse them again with clean water.

Making the Wine

Making flower wines is quite different from making fruit ones. To begin with, assuming you are using a can of concentrated grape juice as the base for the wine, start a fermentation with diluted grape juice and sufficient sugar to produce a medium sweet wine (about one pound) in a bucket. When it is fermenting well, but after the vigorous first ferment has abated, add the flower heads in a straining bag weighted down with a sterilized stone or glass marbles. The reason for placing the flowers inside a straining bag is to prevent them all floating to the top and therefore not having the maximum amount of flavour and aroma extracted.

Leave the flowers in the must for about a week, pressing them gently with a wooden spoon each day to squeeze out as much essence as possible. At the end of this infusion period remove the bag of flower heads and transfer the must to a fermentation jar, fit an airlock and place the jar in a warm spot to ferment to completion. The rest of the procedure is exactly as for fruit wines and wines made from grape juice concentrates.

As with fruits, you can make flower wines from dried flowers, a large variety of which are sold by health shops and herbalists as well as home wine making suppliers. Generally, two ounces of the dried flower heads are sufficient to make a gallon of wine and many wine making suppliers sell them in this quantity sealed in small polythene bags to preserve them.

The procedure for making wine from dried flowers is exactly the same as for fresh flowers.

Vermouth

An interesting variation on flower wines is vermouth. Commercial vermouth is made from fermented grape juice which is flavoured with a blend of herbs, roots and flowers after which it is fortified with added alcohol in the form of spirit. But you can make a very acceptable vermouth at home either by using a blend of dried herbs sold specifically for the purpose or by using a liquid essence of these herbs which is also sold by wine making suppliers. If you use the dried herbs, the method for producing vermouth is exactly the same as for making other wines with dried flowers. But if you use the essence you simply add the prescribed amount to the wine. If you wish to fortify it you can do so by adding a flavourless spirit such as vodka or Polish spirit to the wine to produce a total alcohol content of around twenty per cent. Do this before the wine is left to mature and the result will be a smooth, palatable vermouth which you can drink with great enjoyment. I shall have more to say about fortifying wines in Chapter 7.

The best types of yeast to use for vermouth are Sherry, Madeira, or Tokay. Red or white concentrated grape juice, depending on your preference, make the ideal base for a vermouth, but you can also use fruit wines such as orange, apricot or plum. Remember it is the herbs that give the vermouth its characteristic flavour, not the base wine.

Vegetable Wines

Vegetable wines are not now as popular as they once were, due probably to the increasing availability of fruit pulps and concentrated juices. But some vegetable wines still have a lot to recommend them, in particular those made from potatoes and parsnips.

Wines made from root vegetables always need the addition of chopped raisins or concentrated grape juice in order to give them a degree of vinosity. Without this they tend to be rather dull and flat. It is also essential to add citric acid.

Scrub the roots well and remove any rotten parts, but do not peel them. Chop the vegetables into inch cubes and simmer them with a small piece of crushed root ginger and, if you like, a few cloves, until they are tender. But do not simmer them too long or they will become soft and can cause the wine to become hazy.

Strain the vegetables into a bucket and add the sugar, raisins or grape juice, citric acid, nutrient, and a suitable yeast such as Sherry. Cover the bucket and allow to ferment for two to three days then strain into a fermentation jar, fit an airlock and place in the airing cupboard to ferment to completion. The rest of the procedure is as for fruit and flower wines.

Incidentally, if you simmer your vegetables just before a meal, when you strain the liquid off them you can serve them with a casserole; the spicy flavour given by the ginger and cloves makes them quite delicious.

Other vegetables

You can make wine from just about any vegetable: peas, broad beans, cabbages, lettuces, and the almost legendary pea pod wine.

The procedure is almost identical to that used for wines from root vegetables except, of course, that you need to simmer the vegetables for rather longer than root vegetables for them to become soft. But in this case you ferment on the vegetables as well as on the raisins or grape juice to extract the maximum flavour, colour and aroma. And you should use a tablespoon of pectozyme to help this extraction and to produce a clear, bright wine.

The initial fermentation on the vegetables should last for about a week. At the end of this time strain off all the pulp and transfer the liquid to a fermentation jar. Fit an airlock and proceed as usual.

Mead

Before finishing this chapter on home made wines from fresh ingredients, I must mention a great favourite of mine: mead. This is, of course, a very ancient drink made from honey with citric acid and tannin added and is preferably fermented on a special mead yeast.

The preparation of mead is simplicity itself. You simply bring the honey to the boil in about four pints of water and simmer it gently for about twenty minutes to allow any impurities to float to the surface. Skim the impurities off the surface, allow it to cool and add the acid, a cup of cold tea as tannin (or a few drops of concentrated tannin), a yeast nutrient, and the yeast. Make up to the full gallon with boiled, cooled water, fit a fermentation lock, and leave it to ferment to completion.

Depending on whether you make a sweet or dry mead, you can use it as a dessert wine or as a table wine; it is quite superb with pork or chicken. You can use virtually any honey for making mead and the flavour will vary delicately according to which type of flowers your honey was made from. But these differences will be very subtle and you will find that they are all equally enjoyable. But try to avoid the dark honeys because they tend to give too strong a flavour which can be rather overpowering.

To get the best out of your mead try to resist drinking it for at least a year after you have bottled it, and preferably two years. When you taste it at the end of that time you will be glad you did.

There are all sorts of stories about the therapeutic, medicinal and general restorative properties of honey and mead and if these are true, so much the better. But as for me, I am quite content to enjoy it for what it is — a most acceptable drink.

5 Some Recipes

The last chapter was intended to show in general terms how to make successful wines from fresh ingredients, and as you will have seen, the basic methods are similar. Now here are some recipes for producing good wines. In order to avoid repetition, the detailed instructions are as described in the last chapter.

Fruit Wines

Apple
This makes a delicious light, dry table wine since the apples take on the flavour of the yeast well.

    7lb Bramley apples (windfalls are ideal)
    1½–2lb sugar to give an initial specific gravity of 1·085
    2 teaspoons citric acid
    1 tablespoon pectic enzyme
    5 drops tannin OR ½ cup cold tea
    1 yeast nutrient tablet
    1 gallon water
    Niersteiner or hock yeast

Use the basic method described in Chapter 4, fermenting on the pulp for three days after soaking for twenty-four hours and crushing the fruit. Then strain into a fermentation jar and ferment under an airlock in a warm place.

Dried apricot
A good dessert wine if served rather on the sweet side.

    1lb dried apricots
    2½–3lb sugar to give an initial specific gravity of 1·115
    1 teaspoon citric acid
    5 drops tannin
    1 tablespoon pectic enzyme
    1 yeast nutrient tablet
    1 gallon water
    Sauterne or Tokay yeast

Some fruit which is particularly good for wine making

Soak the apricots for twelve hours in cold water, strain, chop, then follow the basic method. Ferment on the pulp for two days then strain and ferment under airlock. Feed the yeast with small amounts of sugar towards the end of fermentation.

Blackberry

This is a lovely full-bodied table wine that goes down a treat with a good, rich casserole.

    4lb blackberries
    2–2½lb sugar to give an initial specific gravity of 1·090
    1 teaspoon citric acid
    10 drops tannin
    1 tablespoon pectic enzyme
    1 yeast nutrient tablet
    1 gallon water
    Burgundy yeast

Follow basic method, fermenting on the pulp for three days to extract the maximum flavour and colour. Strain and ferment under an airlock to dryness.

You can also make a port-like dessert wine by using more sugar plus raisins or grape juice concentrate.

4lb blackberries
3–3¼lb sugar to give an initial specific gravity of 1·125
4oz chopped raisins OR ¼pt concentrated red grape juice
1 teaspoon citric acid
10 drops tannin
1 tablespoon pectic enzyme
1 yeast nutrient tablet
1 gallon water
Port yeast

Method is as for blackberry table wine, but feed the yeast with small amounts of sugar as fermentation dies down to give a strong sweetish wine.

Blackcurrant

Blackcurrants have a high degree of natural acidity which needs to be offset by the addition of a sweetening agent. For this reason it is best to make these berries into a sweetish port-type wine.

3lb blackcurrants, stalks removed
3–3¼lb sugar to give an initial specific gravity of 1.125
1 tablespoon pectic enzyme
1 yeast nutrient tablet
1 gallon water
Port yeast

The method is exactly the same as for blackberry wine, but do not forget to keep the fermentation going for as long as possible by adding small amounts of sugar at regular intervals.

Morello Cherry

A strong medium-sweet to sweet wine which makes a beautiful dessert wine.

4lb Morello cherries

3¼–3½lb sugar to give initial specific gravity of 1·135
2 teaspoons citric acid
10 drops tannin
1 tablespoon pectic enzyme
1 yeast nutrient tablet
1 gallon water
Madeira or Sauterne yeast

Follow basic method. Ferment on the pulp for two days then strain and ferment under airlock. Feed the yeast with small amounts of sugar towards the end of fermentation. This will then produce a strong medium-sweet to sweet wine.

If you like cherries to have an almond flavour, crack a few of the cherry stones and include them in the pulp while fermenting, but only add a dozen or so or the almond taste may become overpowering.

Damson port

This is one of my real favourites. It produces a strong wine that is full of flavour and forms the ideal accompaniment to Stilton cheese after a meal.

4lb damsons
3–3½lb sugar to give initial specific gravity of 1·135
2 teaspoons citric acid
10 drops tannin
1 tablespoon pectic enzyme
1 yeast nutrient tablet
1 gallon water
Port yeast

Follow basic method. Ferment on the pulp for four to five days to extract the maximum amount of flavour and colour. Strain and ferment under airlock. As with the morello cherry wine, if the wine ferments to dryness, feed the yeast with a little sugar at a time until fermentation stops and adjust the final specific gravity to about 1·015.

When you strain the pulp for this wine, do not throw it away — return it to the bucket and add a 1lb of chopped raisins and sufficient sugar to give an initial specific gravity of 1·090 (about 2 pounds) plus the same amount of citric acid, tannin and pectic enzyme and yeast nutrient that you used for the port recipe – and make a second gallon of wine, fermenting on a Burgundy or Bordeaux yeast to produce a dryish table wine that goes well with duck or turkey.

Elderberry

This is one of the traditional favourites among home wine makers, although not, I fear, with this particular home wine maker!

2lb elderberries
2¼–2½lb sugar to give an initial specific gravity of 1·090
2 teaspoons citric acid
1 tablespoon pectic enzyme
1 yeast nutrient tablet
1 gallon water
Burgundy yeast

(Since elderberries are rich in tannin, you do not need to add any extra in the form of concentrate or cold tea. In fact, if the elderberries are only newly ripened you may find your wine has a rather harsh character initially, but this should disappear during maturing, especially if you allow it to mature for a year or more.)

Follow the basic method, fermenting on the pulp for four days. Strain into a fermentation jar, fit an airlock, and ferment to dryness. If you increase the amount of sugar to about 3½ pounds (to give an initial specific gravity of 1·135), add half a pound of chopped raisins and use the same amount of citric acid, pectic enzyme and nutrient, you can make a good port-type wine by fermenting on a port yeast. Use the method as for elderberry table wine, but feed the yeast with extra sugar towards the end of the fermentation to ensure that you get a strong, sweetish wine. You will need to keep it for a year to eighteen months before drinking to allow the wine to mellow and lose any harshness.

This is another case where you can make a second gallon of wine from the already fermented pulp since elderberries contain a lot of flavour and colour as well as tannin.

Gooseberry

5lb gooseberries
2¼–2½lb sugar to give an initial specific gravity of 1·095
½lb chopped raisins
OR ½pt white grape juice concentrate
2 teaspoons citric acid
5 drops tannin
1 tablespoon pectic enzyme
1 yeast nutrient tablet
1 gallon water
Chablis, hock or Niersteiner yeast

Make sure you remove all stalks from the gooseberries then follow the basic method. Ferment on the pulp for a week, then strain into a fermentation jar, fit an airlock and ferment to dryness. Allow this wine to mature for about a year, after which time it will closely resemble the type of wine according to which yeast you used.

If you like sparkling wine, you can make a good imitation Champagne with gooseberries using the ingredients and method I have just described but with only 1½ to 2 pounds of sugar and using a Champagne yeast. When the wine clears, bottle it, preferably in Champagne bottles, add a teaspoon of sugar to each bottle and secure the corks with wire.

Incidentally, for both of these gooseberrry wines use the berries when they are green and hard rather than when they become soft and juicy. The reason for this is that the ripe gooseberries retain their strong flavour which comes over rather overpoweringly in the finished wine.

Loganberry

A delicious table wine and an ideal accompaniment to duck or turkey.

2lb loganberries
2–2½lb sugar to give an initial specific gravity of 1.090
8oz chopped raisins OR ½pt concentrated red grape juice
1 teaspoon citric acid
10 drops tannin

1 tablespoon pectic enzyme
1 yeast nutrient tablet
1 gallon water
Bordeaux yeast

Follow the basic method, fermenting on the pulp for three to four days to make sure that all the flavour and colour have been extracted from the fruit. Strain and ferment under airlock to dryness.

Orange

10 oranges, average size (preferably half Seville oranges and half sweet oranges)
$2\frac{1}{2}$–$2\frac{3}{4}$lb sugar to give an initial specific gravity of 1·110
8oz chopped raisins or sultanas
OR $\frac{1}{2}$pt concentrated white grape juice
1 teaspoon citric acid
5 drops tannin
1 tablespoon pectic enzyme

1 tablet yeast nutrient
1 gallon water
Sherry or Sauterne yeast

Thinly peel the oranges and chop them then follow the basic method. Ferment on the pulp for four days and strain into a fermentation jar before fermenting under an airlock. Serve medium sweet as a table wine or ferment out to dryness by feeding the yeast with added sugar in the later stages of fermentation and serve almost, but not quite, dry as an aperitif. Served either way, I find orange wine really delicious and very easy to make.

Peach

This is an ideal wine to make during the summer, when the fruit is plentiful and relatively cheap. A superb light table wine and an ideal accompaniment to chicken.

3lb ripe peaches – stoned and chopped
1¾–2lb sugar to give an initial specific gravity of 1.090
8oz chopped raisins OR ½pt concentrated white grape juice
1 teaspoon citric acid
5 drops tannin
1 tablespoon pectic enzyme
1 yeast nutrient tablet
1 gallon water
Chablis yeast

Ferment on the pulp for three days before straining into a jar to ferment under airlock until dry.

Pear

A delicious light, dry table wine to accompany pork or veal.

4lb ripe pears
2¼–2½lb sugar to give a specific gravity of 1.100
8oz chopped raisins OR ½pt concentrated white grape juice
1 teaspoon citric acid
5 drops tannin

1 tablespoon pectic enzyme
1 yeast nutrient tablet
1 gallon water
Niersteiner or hock yeast

Chop the pears and soak in water for twenty-four hours then add the rest of the ingredients and ferment on the pulp for three days. Strain into a fermentation jar and ferment under airlock until dry.

Plum

5lb Victoria plums
2–2¼lb sugar to give an initial specific gravity of 1·095
1 teaspoon citric acid
5 drops tannin
1 tablespoon pectic enzyme
1 yeast nutrient tablet
1 gallon water
Bordeaux or Burgundy yeast

Follow the basic method, fermenting on the pulp for four days. Strain into a fermentation jar, fit an airlock and ferment to dryness. This makes a really delicious dry table wine with a delicate pink colour and it is an ideal accompaniment to roast pork.

You can, if you like, make a second gallon from the used pulp by adding a pound of chopped raisins and proceeding in the same way as for the 'second pressing' damson wine.

Prune

2lb prunes
2¾–3lb sugar to give an initial specific gravity of 1·120
8oz chopped raisins
OR ½pt concentrated white grape juice
1 teaspoon citric acid
10 drops tannin
1 tablespoon pectic enzyme
1 yeast nutrient tablet
1 gallon water
Madeira or Tokay yeast

Soak the prunes for twelve hours in cold water. Strain, chop, remove stones and follow basic method. Ferment on the pulp for two days then strain and ferment under airlock. In the later stages of fermentation feed the yeast with extra sugar to make the wine as strong as possible and serve rather sweet.

Raisin

1lb raisins, chopped
$1\frac{1}{4}$–$1\frac{3}{4}$lb sugar to give an initial specific gravity of 1·080
1 teaspoon citric acid
5 drops tannin
1 tablespoon pectic enzyme
1 yeast nutrient tablet
1 gallon water
Niersteiner or hock yeast

Follow basic method, fermenting on the pulp for about five days. Strain into a fermentation jar and ferment under airlock to dryness. This produces a wine which is very like the light German table wines and it has a true 'winey' taste. You can vary the amount of sugar to produce sweeter wines or stronger dry wines if you wish, and by increasing the amount of raisins to two or three pounds you can make a very acceptable dessert wine. But in this case feed the yeast with sugar towards the end of fermentation to produce a strong medium sweet to sweet result.

You can also produce similar wines using sultanas instead of raisins.

Rhubarb

The best time to make this wine is in late May when the fruit is ripest – the stalks must be red.

6lb ripe rhubarb
2–$2\frac{1}{4}$lb sugar to give an initial specific gravity of 1.090
1lb chopped raisins OR 1pt concentrated white grape juice
1 teaspoon citric acid
5 drops tannin
1 yeast nutrient tablet

1 gallon water
Hock yeast

Rhubarb contains a high percentage of oxalic acid which must be neutralised before you can start making the wine. This is done by chopping the fruit and pouring over it half of the water, boiling it, then when it has cooled, stirring in one ounce of precipitated chalk. Leave for two days, then follow the standard method. Ferment on the pulp for two days before straining into a jar to ferment to dryness. This makes a really superb table wine. But do not be in too much of a hurry to drink it; it gets better the longer you keep it.

Flower Wines

One of the big advantages of making flower wines is that if you like them you can make them throughout the spring, summer and early autumn since there always seems to be some sort of flower in bloom from March right through to September.

Because flowers are used simply as a flavouring and colouring agent when making wine, the method and individual recipes vary even less than they do with fruit wines. So really, all you need to know is the quantity of flower heads you need in order to flavour the wine of your choice.

Here, then, are the quantities you need for a variety of flower wines.

Broom

Two quarts of flowers.

Clover

Two quarts of the purple flower heads.

Coltsfoot

Two quarts – you may find this wine improved if you crush a small piece of root ginger and add it to the straining bag with the flowers while infusing.

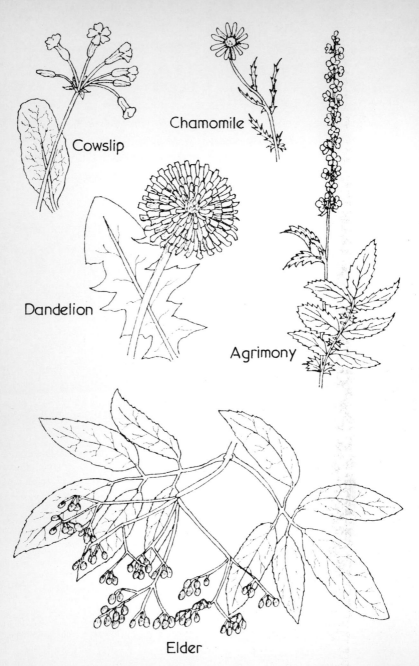

Cowslip

Chamomile

Dandelion

Agrimony

Elder

Wines can be made from the fruits, flowers, leaves or roots of most non-poisonous plants

Cowslip

Two to three quarts. Be particularly careful not to get any green parts in the infusion since they will make the wine rather bitter.

Dandelion

Two quarts. In this case a few green parts left in will do no harm and can even be beneficial if you allow the wine to mature for two to three years before you drink it. After this time the flavour bears a striking resemblence to Scotch!

Elderflower

You need very few elderflowers to flavour a wine and if you use too many the bouquet can become decidedly unpleasant — rather reminiscent of tom cats — so use only one pint of flower heads for this wine and be sure to remove all green parts.

Gorse

You need four quarts of these golden blossoms since they have a rather delicate flavour.

Hawthorn blossom

Two quarts of pink or white hawthorn flowers.

Honeysuckle

These flowers are very strongly scented and you need only one quart to make a wine. Again, be sure to get rid of all the green parts and leaves.

Marigold

Two quarts of flowers.

Primrose

Two to three quarts are necessary as these flowers are rather delicately scented.

Rose petals

Use two quarts of dark red petals for a red wine or the same amount of white or yellow petals if you prefer a pale golden wine. Lovers of flower wines consider this to be one of the most delicious of all.

Although not strictly a flower wine, you can also make a rather interesting wine from two quarts of oak leaves when they first open out in spring.

Vegetable Wines

Beetroot

    5lb beetroot
    3–3¼lb sugar to give an initial specific gravity of 1·125
    2 teaspoons citric acid
    15 drops tannin
    1 tablespoon pectic enzyme
    1 yeast nutrient tablet
    6 cloves
    1 small piece root ginger, crushed
    1 gallon water
    Port or Madeira yeast

Follow basic method for making vegetable wines which I gave in Chapter 4 and towards the end of fermentation under an airlock feed the yeast with small amounts of sugar to produce a wine which is medium sweet. Allow it to mature for two years if possible.

Broad bean

    4lb shelled broad beans (preferably old, hard ones)
    2½–2¾lb sugar to give an initial specific gravity of 1·100
    4oz chopped raisins
    OR ¼pt concentrated white grape juice
    2 teaspoons citric acid
    10 drops tannin
    1 tablespoon pectic enzyme
    1 yeast nutrient tablet
    1 gallon water
    Hock or Niersteiner yeast

Follow the basic method and ferment under an airlock until dry. Mature in the bottle for twelve months. This makes a very good light table wine which is the ideal accompaniment to chicken or fish.

Carrot

    4lb carrots (good quality)
    3¼–3½lb sugar to give an initial specific gravity of 1·135
    8oz chopped raisins
    OR ½pt concentrated white grape juice
    2 teaspoons citric acid
    10 drops tannin
    1 tablespoon pectic enzyme
    1 yeast nutrient tablet
    1 gallon water
    Sherry yeast

Follow the basic method and feed the yeast with small amounts of sugar towards the end of fermentation under lock. This wine is best served medium sweet to sweet.

Marrow

    4lb ripe marrow
    2¾–3lb sugar to give an initial specific gravity of 1·110
    4oz chopped raisins
    OR ¼pt concentrated white grape juice
    1 small piece root ginger, crushed
    2 teaspoons citric acid
    10 drops tannin
    1 tablespoon pectic enzyme
    1 yeast nutrient tablet
    1 gallon water
    Sherry or Madeira yeast

Follow the basic method, chopping the marrow into small pieces or grating it coarsely and including the seeds. Ferment on the pulp for four to five days then strain into a fermentation jar, fit an airlock and stand in a warm spot to ferment to completion.

Parsnip

5lb parsnips
2¾–3lb sugar to give an initial specific gravity of 1·115
8oz chopped raisins
OR ½pt concentrated white grape juice
2 teaspoons citric acid
10 drops tannin
1 tablespoon pectic enzyme
1 yeast nutrient tablet
1 gallon water
Sherry or Madeira yeast

The best type of parsnips to use for this wine are those which have been bitten by a sharp frost.

Follow the basic method and towards the end of fermentation under airlock feed the yeast with sugar a little at a time and allow the wine to mature for at least eighteen months before you drink it. This wine is best served strong and rather sweet. If carefully made and matured it is possibly the best of all country wines.

Pea pod

5lb pea pods (the fresher and younger the better)
2½–2¾lb sugar to give an initial specific gravity of 1·105
4oz chopped raisins
OR ¼pt concentrated white grape juice
2 teaspoons citric acid
5 drops tannin
1 tablespoon pectic enzyme
1 yeast nutrient tablet
1 gallon water
Chablis, Graves, hock or Niersteiner yeast

Follow the basic method and ferment under airlock until completely dry. Mature this wine for about two years.

Despite the perhaps rather unusual main ingredient, pea pod wine has a really delicious light bouquet and flavour which makes it superb as a hock-type table wine. It can also be drunk with real enjoyment at any time of the day.

Potato

3lb old potatoes
3–3¼lb sugar to give an initial specific gravity of 1·120
4oz chopped raisins
OR ¼pt concentrated white grape juice
1 small piece root ginger, crushed
6 cloves
2 teaspoons citric acid
15 drops tannin
1 tablespoon pectic enzyme
1 yeast nutrient tablet
1 gallon water
Sherry or Madeira yeast

Follow the basic recipe, fermenting on the raisins for four to five days. Strain into a fermentation jar and fit an airlock. Feed the yeast with small quantities of sugar towards the end of fermentation to produce a strong, rather sweet wine. This makes a splendid dessert wine which can be enjoyed at any time throughout the day.

. . . and a couple of odd ones

Tea wine

1 gallon cold tea
3–3¼lb sugar to give an initial specific gravity of 1·135
1lb chopped raisins
OR 1pt concentrated white grape juice
1 teaspoon citric acid
1 yeast nutrient tablet
Sherry or Madeira yeast

While you can make this wine by collecting left-over cold tea from the pot, it is far better to use a gallon of fresh tea. Pour the tea over the raisins in a bucket and add the citric acid, yeast nutrient and yeast starter. Ferment on the pulp for a week then strain, pressing the raisins to extract the maximum amount of juice. Ferment under an airlock for as long as possible, feeding the yeast with small amounts of sugar as fermentation slows down. This gives a very good strong, sweet wine which is ideal after a meal.

Coffee wine

   8oz freshly ground coffee
   OR 1 heaped tablespoon instant coffee
   3–3$\frac{1}{4}$lb sugar to give an initial specific gravity of 1·120
   8oz chopped raisins
   OR $\frac{1}{2}$pt concentrated white grape juice
   2 teaspoons citric acid
   1 yeast nutrient tablet
   1 gallon water
   Sherry or general purpose yeast

Make the coffee in the usual way and leave to infuse for about ten minutes. Pour it on to the chopped raisins and add the sugar and citric acid. Allow to cool then add the yeast nutrient and yeast starter. Ferment on the raisins for a week then strain into a fermentation jar, pressing the raisins well to extract all the juice. Ferment under airlock until completion, feeding the yeast with small amounts of sugar towards the end of fermentation. This will give a medium sweet dessert wine which, if you mature it well, has a flavour not unlike a coffee liqueur.

6 Home Brewed Beer

In many ways, brewing your own beer at home is even easier than making your own wine, especially if you take the easy (and sensible) way out and make your beer from a can of ready hopped concentrated wort.

While many home brewers insist that the only real way to make your own beer is by boiling together malt extract, malt grains and dried hops then straining and adding sugar before fermenting, this can take a very long time and the chances of failure are fairly high. When I first brewed my own beer I did, in fact, use this system simply because it was the only way at that time to do the job. But now there are several companies producing cans of concentrated wort, consisting of malt extract mixed with hop extract, or dehydrated wort made from boiling together hops and malt grains. The advantages of these concentrated worts are quite considerable; they take very little time to convert into beer, and they are also extremely simple to use. What is more, the results are usually consistently good and they tend to work out cheaper than preparing your own wort from basic ingredients such as malt grains and dried hops.

Most of the concentrated worts are available in a variety of different types to produce bitter, mild, lager, stout, light ale, and so on, so you can pick the type of beer you like best, buy a suitable can of concentrate and make up a brew with every chance of success. And it is real beer!

These concentrates are usually available in two sizes, to make two gallons or five gallons. It is best to start with one of the small sizes and try the different makes until you find a beer that you really like, then move on to the five gallon size and if you really like your beer start a five gallon production line going. I shall describe how to do this later in the chapter.

Choosing the Concentrate

Cans of concentrate for home brewed beer are generally of two types. One is described as hopped malt extract and the other as

Hops

concentrated brewing wort with hop extract. Of the two, the second is probably the better.

You can buy these products from any home made wine and brewing supplier and from several chemists including Boots branches throughout the country.

As for equipment, you require very little: a polythene bin, preferably with a tap at the bottom, to brew in, a second similar vessel into which you can siphon the beer to clear and mature, and some beer bottles or some form of barrel or keg in which to store the beer ready for drinking. And that is all you need if you make your beer from the concentrated wort. But if you decide to use malt extract type kits you will need something in which to boil the extract with water; a preserving pan is ideal.

The Brewing Process

As with making a wine from concentrated grape juice, I shall describe the method used for brewing from a particular kit. In this case the Unican concentrate. Other makes produce beer which is equally good and follow a similar procedure, but do read the instructions carefully before you start and take account of any small differences in the process with your particular make of concentrate.

Like all fermenting processes, the first thing you must do is sterilize the fermenting vessel using the sodium metabisulphite solution or Campden tablets.

The Unican concentrate comes complete with a sachet of beer yeast of the correct type for the kind of beer you are going to make. It is fixed on to the top of the can with an adhesive. Remove this sachet of yeast from the can and after opening the can, stand it in hot water for about ten minutes to soften the concentrate.

Empty the concentrate into the fermentation vessel. (If you are using a plastic bucket make sure it is either white or of a very light colour for the reasons I gave in the chapter on making wines.) Add two pints of hot water to the bucket, rinsing out the can well with the water first to remove every last drop of concentrate.

Dissolve 1¼lb of white sugar in the hot solution, stirring well, then add 15pts of cold water and the contents of the yeast packet. (This is, of course, assuming that you are making the two gallon

Pour the concentrated wort into a sterilized bucket followed by a proportion of the (heated) water

Add the sugar, stirring to make sure it is all dissolved, then add the remaining (cold) water

Cover with a clean tea towel or polythene sheet and stand in a warm place until fermentation is complete

size.) If your fermentation bucket has a close-fitting lid fit this, or if it has not, cover the bucket with a sheet of polythene or tea towel to prevent any airborne bacteria or foreign matter getting into the brew.

Place the fermentation bucket in an airing cupboard or similar warm place at around 21–26°C (70–80°F) and leave it for three days. If you have nowhere sufficiently warm, you can carry out your brew at room temperature – 16–21°C (60–70°F) – but in this case you will need to leave it for five days.

At the end of the fermentation period pour or preferably siphon the beer from the fermenting bucket into a clean, sterilized plastic bucket, leaving the yeast deposit behind. Since this yeast deposit is of no further use you can discard it.

At this stage, check the specific gravity with your hydrometer. You should get a reading of between 1·010 and 1·000. Cover the bucket with polythene sheet or the close-fitting lid and leave for three days at room temperature. During this time the beer will begin to clear.

When the three days are up, dissolve $2\frac{1}{4}$ to $2\frac{1}{2}$ ounces of white sugar in a cupful of hot water. Pour this into a clean, sterilized plastic bucket (use the one which you used to ferment your beer in or if you have already started another batch, use a fresh bucket) then siphon the beer on to this syrup. Again, leave behind any yeast deposit and throw it away. Stir the mixture well to ensure that the sugar solution is evenly distributed throughout the beer then siphon into half-pint or pint beer bottles and close them with re-useable caps or proper Crown corks. But if you use Crown corks you will, of course, need a capper to crimp the edge of the Crown cork around the neck of the bottle.

Stand the bottles of beer in a warm place – 18–24°C (65–75°F) – for a week to finish clearing. At the end of this time your beer should be really clear and ready for drinking. The sugar solution which you added to the beer before bottling will have caused a small amount of secondary fermentation so that when you open the bottle you will have beer with a natural sparkle which should form a good firm head when you pour it into your glass.

And that is all there is to it!

Keeping Beer in Bulk

If you prefer to have your beer on draught, as it were, instead of in bottles, there are a number of special pressure kegs now available on the market in which you can store the beer until you are ready to drink it. These kegs all use carbon dioxide Sparklets bulbs to provide the pressure which keeps the natural fermentation gases in the beer and to carbonate the brew to give it a sparkle.

As the level of the beer goes down in the keg, obviously the pressure decreases. You can replenish this pressure by letting in more carbon dioxide from the Sparklets bulb. In this way the beer retains its natural conditioning and the last pint is in just as good condition and with just as good a head as the first pint. The big advantage of using this method for keeping draught beer is that no air is allowed into the keg and so the beer will be in perfect condition for several months if need be.

One of these five gallon kegs, used in conjunction with two five gallon fermenting buckets, makes the ideal set-up for a five gallon

A typical two gallon beer kit including a suitable yeast

production line which will ensure that you always have some beer on tap ready to drink.

The Production Line

If you are very fond of beer and you have found a concentrated wort that produces a brew that you really like, it is well worthwhile starting up a five gallon production line; this really is very simple.

All you need are two five gallon fermenting vessels, and a five gallon pressurized storage keg. At any one time you have five gallons of beer brewing in the first fermentation vessel, you have five gallons clearing and maturing in the second vessel, and you have five gallons on tap ready to drink in the pressurized storage keg.

Always use proper beer bottles as they are designed to withstand the pressure of secondary fermentation. In front of the bottles are (*l*) plastic closures, and (*r*) crown corks with a simple hand device for fitting them

When you have emptied the keg you fill it again from the second fermentation vessel with beer which has by this time cleared and matured. Then you transfer the five gallons from the first fermentation vessel into the second and start a new brew in the first vessel.

You can keep this cycle going indefinitely, and when your friends drop in you can always be sure you will have a pint of foaming home brew which you can offer them.

The Bag Boy Brewer

For those who are about to start brewing beer for the first time, a company called Bar Made Limited have introduced an ingenious product which is, in effect, a complete brewery in a box. It consists of two collapsible cages into which fit two plastic and nylon laminated food grade quality bags, two combined caps and taps, and a length of plastic tubing. The whole kit enables you to brew and dispense your beer in a totally closed system. This means that at no time does the beer come into contact with the air and this eliminates all the problems of contamination as well as getting rid of separate fermenting vessels, siphon tube, bottles, caps and pressure vessels or kegs which require gas injectors and a supply of Sparklets bulbs which are rather expensive.

In principle, the Bag Boy Brewer is very simple. The beer, which can be any type you like, is fermented in one of the plastic and nylon bags which is connected to the other bag by the length of tubing; it joins the two taps together. Carbon dioxide gas produced during fermentation fills the top of the fermentation bag and then travels through the tube and begins to inflate the empty bag.

When fermentation has finished, you disconnect the empty bag and press as much of the carbon dioxide out of it as you can. Then you reconnect the tube and transfer the beer from the fermentation bag into the empty bag. The way you do this is simplicity itself. You merely press down on top of the fermentation bag and the beer is forced out through the tube into the other one. But before transferring the beer you pour a sugar syrup solution into the empty bag to give the secondary fermentation which produces a natural sparkle in the beer.

Once the beer is in the second bag, you leave it for a few days to allow the syrup to cause the secondary fermentation which will fill the top of the bag with carbon dioxide gas again.

When you dispense the beer from the second bag, you keep the tap just below the level of the beer so that you are drawing the beer from the top where it is clear rather than from the bottom where you could disturb any cloudy deposit. And by keeping the tap just below the level of the beer you ensure that the carbon dioxide formed during secondary fermentation remains in the top of the bag.

As you draw the beer off, the bag gradually collapses but the carbon dioxide remains in position. The outcome of all this is that your beer is brewed, conditioned and dispensed with the protective cap of carbon dioxide gas over it at all stages – it never comes into contact with the air.

As you will have seen from this chapter, brewing your own beer at home is a very simple procedure, but I have, of course, only dealt with it on the surface, showing you a way to produce good beer quickly, cheaply, and without involving a lot of your spare time. However, if you feel that you want to delve deeper into the processes and procedures of making beers from basic ingredients, then you will have to look further afield than this book. There are several very good books on the market which deal in great depth with home brewing and I have listed some of these in the bibliography at the end of this book. But of course, if you are looking for a simple, foolproof method of making good beer without spending too much time, you can do no better than using the concentrated brewing wort that is freely available in cans.

7 Bottling and Blending

The last thing that you do to your wine before you actually drink it is to rack it into bottles for storage and this is the stage at which you can make or break an otherwise good wine. You can make it by bottling your wine in proper wine bottles which have been thoroughly cleaned and sterilized and then fitting corks, capsules and labels to give a final professional touch. You can just as easily break a good wine by being careless over cleaning and sterilizing your bottles and by putting the wine into old lemonade, orange squash or tonic water bottles. But before we get on to the actual procedure for bottling let us look at the preparation work you must do first.

Stabilizing your Wine

Your wine is ready for bottling when it is clear and bright and when it has dropped virtually no lees after the last time you racked it into a clean storage jar. If there is a considerable deposit at the bottom of the storage jar, play safe and rack it again into another clean storage jar and leave it for another couple of months or so. It will certainly do the wine no harm and may make all the difference between a good wine and a great one.

But assuming that your wine is clear and there is no lees deposited at the bottom of the jar, stabilize the wine by adding a final crushed Campden tablet to it. Allow the wine to stand for a day or two after you have added this stabilizing tablet before you bottle the wine. This will give it time to dissolve properly and infiltrate the wine.

Preparing the Bottles

Always use good, sound wine bottles of the appropriate type for your home made wines. There are several different types of bottle of various colours and shapes, each of which is traditionally used for a particular type of wine. For example, white wines are often bottled in clear glass or greenish glass bottles so that their delicate colour and brightness can be easily appreciated. The only excep-

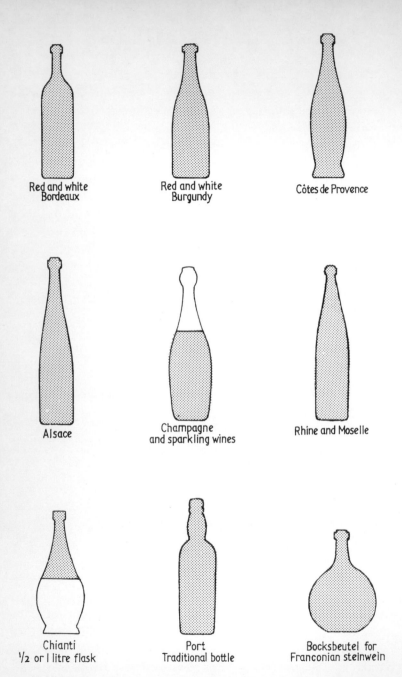

Red and white
Bordeaux

Red and white
Burgundy

Côtes de Provence

Alsace

Champagne
and sparkling wines

Rhine and Moselle

Chianti
1/2 or l litre flask

Port
Traditional bottle

Bocksbeutel for
Franconian steinwein

Standard bottles for wine

tions to this are the German wines which are usually bottled in dark brown or green bottles.

Red wines, on the other hand, are nearly always contained in dark green or brown bottles. The reason for this is simply that the rich red colour of the wine is affected by light and if the wine stands in light for too long the colour can become a rather unpleasant brown.

So the first general rule that it is advisable to follow is to put your red wines into dark green bottles and your white ones into clear or very pale green bottles. If you want to make the presentation of your wines as professional as possible, it is a good idea to try to use bottles of the correct shape as well as colour. Burgundy type wines, which include elderberry and damson as well as those made from concentrated red grape juice, with a Burgundy yeast, should go into dark green bottles with sloping shoulders while those wines which have been fermented on Chablis or Graves yeasts should be bottled in containers of the same shape but in clear or greenish glass. If you have any wines which you have fermented on a Bordeaux or Claret yeast, these should be bottled in the traditional Bordeaux shaped bottle which is straight-sided and square-shouldered.

Wines which are of the hock, Niersteiner or Mosel types are best stored in the tall tapering brown or green bottles which the Germans traditionally use for their white wines. And if you have made Port, Madeira or Sherry type wines then these should go into any of the bottles in which these drinks are normally purchased.

The main difference between bottles for dessert wines and those for table wines is that the table wine bottles are 'punted'. This simply means that they have an inverted indentation in the bottom of the bottle, the purpose of which is to allow any remaining sediment to collect in the corner of the bottle, as it were, rather than spreading itself evenly all over the bottom. Dessert wine bottles, on the other hand, are flat-bottomed.

Always use Champagne bottles for sparkling wines because these are specially designed and made to withstand the pressure which is generated by the secondary fermentation inside the bottle. They also have a specially shaped neck which enables you to wire the cork on easily and safely.

Most wine bottles have a capacity of about 70 to 75 centilitres which means that you can get just under a gallon of wine into six of them. Exceptions to this are Champagne bottles which normally hold rather more and you will find that a gallon goes comfortably into five of these bottles. Litre bottles are also becoming more popular and you can put any table wine into these; you will find that you can fill four from a gallon and have about half a litre left over which you can put into a half-bottle; what's left after that you can sample!

When you are ready to bottle your wine, collect the bottles you are going to use and give them a thorough washing inside and out to remove any dirt, dust and old sediment. The best way to do this is by using a bottle brush on the inside and giving a good wash by hand on the outside.

Never, never wash bottles in water to which washing-up liquid has been added. No matter how thoroughly you rinse the bottles afterwards you never seem to be able to get rid of a trace of unpleasant detergent flavour in your wines. So always wash your wine bottles – and your wine glasses, come to that – in plain hot water.

When you have washed the bottles sterilize them using the standard sodium metabisulphite or Campden tablet solution, and place them upside down on a rack to drain. Incidentally, when you are washing your bottles be particularly careful to remove all traces of old labels and gum from them. While this will in no way affect the quality and taste of your wine, it can spoil an otherwise professional presentation.

You must also carefully sterilize the corks you are going to use. And here again it is best to try to use the correct cork for the type of wine you are bottling. Traditionally, table wine bottles are fitted with straight-sided cylindrical corks which are sunk into the bottle so that the top is flush with the top of the bottle itself. This type of cork has to be inserted with a special device which I shall describe shortly. Dessert wine bottles are invariably fitted with flanged corks which are easily fitted and removed by hand. This is because while a bottle of table wine is usually drunk at one sitting during a meal, dessert wines are consumed in smaller quantities and are required to last rather longer. Therefore the cork is likely to be

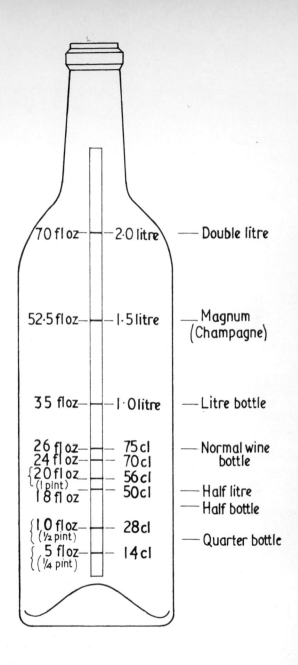

70 fl oz — 2·0 litre — Double litre

52·5 fl oz — 1·5 litre — Magnum (Champagne)

35 fl oz — 1·0 litre — Litre bottle

26 fl oz — 75 cl — Normal wine bottle
24 fl oz — 70 cl
{20 fl oz (1 pint) — 56 cl — Half litre
18 fl oz — 50 cl — Half bottle

{10 fl oz (½ pint) — 28 cl — Quarter bottle

{5 fl oz (¼ pint) — 14 cl

Bottle Capacities

To bottle your wine, use a siphon tube, keeping the end well above the lees in the bottom of the demijohn

inserted and removed from the bottle several times.

Many wine makers are turning to polythene closures which are similar in shape to the traditional corks because they are easy to sterilize and reuse. But somehow, to me at least, this seems a retrograde step so while I may be accused of flying in the face of progress I have so far refused to change over to these modern contraptions. But looked at logically they are certainly in no way inferior to the traditional corks and in many ways they must be better. However, whichever type of closure you decide to use, sterilize them thoroughly in sodium metabisulphite or Campden tablet solution immediately before inserting them in the bottle, and do not rinse them after you have sterilized them. The best way is to put the corks into a basin of the sterilizing solution and allow them to soak for several hours. In this condition they will enter the neck of the bottle fairly easily and will immediately form a good seal.

Filling the Bottles

The only pieces of equipment you need for bottling your wine are a siphon tube with a U-tube fitting on the end, as I described in Chapter 2, and a hand corking machine or corking gun with which to fit the straight-sided corks to your table wine bottles.

Again, the first step in this bottling process is the obvious one — to sterilize the siphon tube to prevent any contamination with bacteria or off-flavours from wines which you have previously bottled. The easiest way to sterilize the siphon is by sucking the solution through the tube. But be very careful not to get it into your mouth because it is a very unpleasant taste which takes a long time to get rid of. When you have sterilized the tube allow it to drain thoroughly so that you do not suck any of the sterilizing solution which may be left in the tube into your mouth when you start to siphon the wine.

Place the storage container with your wine in it on a convenient working surface about three feet from the ground and insert the siphon tube into the jar. Many siphon tubes have a long glass tube with the U-shaped section at the bottom. The long glass tube fits through a cork which in turn fits into the neck of the storage jar. This enables you to adjust the depth of the siphon tube so that you

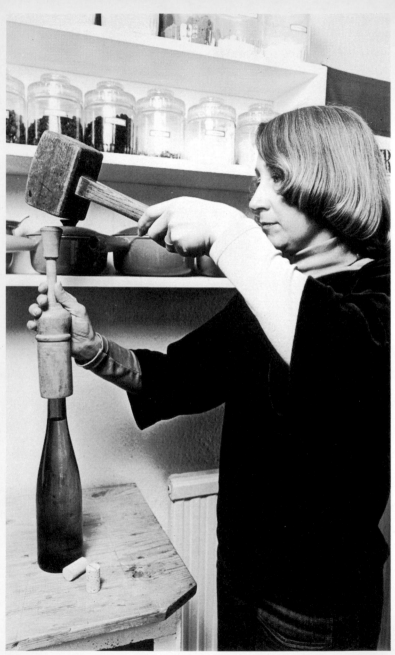

Corking is easily carried out with a corking gun

are continually drawing wine from just below the surface. However, if you have one of these siphon tubes it is a good idea to cut a small v along the length of the cork where it fits into the neck of the jar to allow air to enter the jar to replace the wine which you have siphoned out. In some cases, if you do not do this, a vacuum is built up inside the storage jar which will prevent the wine siphoning out and into your bottles.

Stand the bottles on the floor beneath the storage jar and suck the wine through the siphon tube to start the flow. Insert the tube into the neck of each bottle in turn and fill the bottles to within about an inch of where the bottom of the cork is going to be. I usually allow the wine to run down the inside of the bottle rather than just pouring straight into the bottom. This avoids the wine frothing and absorbing too much air; I believe that the correct time for a wine to absorb air is when you open it just before serving.

When all the bottles are full, insert the corks using either a hand corking machine or a wooden or plastic corking gun if you are using straight-sided corks. The principle of these corkers is very simple. They consist of a tapered metal tube into which you place the cork. This then fits over the neck of the bottle and you either press a lever which forces the cork down the tapered tube, where it is compressed, and into the neck of the bottle, or, in the corking gun, you strike the top of the device with a wooden mallet and this again forces the cork down the tapered tube and into the neck of the bottle.

If you intend to store your wine in the bottles for a considerable time, it is a good idea to seal the top of the cork and the joint between the cork and the neck of the bottle with a little melted candle wax to prevent any chance of air entering through the cork if it should become dried out.

Finish off the job of bottling by fitting foil or plastic capsules over the top of the cork and the neck of the bottle. This gives a really professional finish to your wine and since they are available in various colours – usually red, white, gold and silver – you can use them to identify the type of wine contained in the bottle. You can also buy capsules made of a viscose material which, in addition to making the bottle of wine look very attractive, also provide an airtight seal and do, therefore, the same job as the melted candle

Foil capsules give your wine a professional finish

wax. These viscose capsules are fitted to the bottle while wet and as they dry out they shrink to form the seal.

The final step in bottling is to fix labels to your bottles of wine. Again you can do this simply by using plain white labels and writing the type of wine on with a ball-point pen, or you can do the job properly and use labels which are specially made for bottles of home made wine. The second method is, of course, by far the better because it again helps to give your wine an attractive appearance in the bottle. Most wine making suppliers stock labels in a wide variety of different styles, some printed with wine names and others plain for writing your own. I prefer the printed type, but if your handwriting is neat the plain type can give just as good a result.

Storing your Wine

Wines should always be stored in a fairly cool, dark place where the temperature does not change very much throughout the year; a cellar is, of course, ideal. The ideal way is to store the bottles on their sides in proper wine racks. These are designed to tip the bottles almost horizontal but with the base very slightly lower than the neck. In this way the cork stays moistened by the wine but any small amount of sediment which may drop out of the wine falls to the bottom and settles round the punt.

Although it is generally thought that all wines improve with keeping, this is not necessarily true. Table wines, especially light dry ones, reach their peak after about six months to a year; two years at the most. After this they gradually begin to deteriorate and after a few more years can become quite undrinkable. When you have spent time and money producing these wines, it would be a pity not to be able to drink them! Sweeter, heavier dessert wines, however, do tend to improve with keeping. But again I would suggest that five years is probably the time by which they should be drunk.

Blending

Occasionally you may produce a gallon of wine which does not come up to expectations; it may be too sweet, it may be flat and lifeless. Or it may just not taste right. You can usually improve

Apply a label to each bottle as a finishing touch

such wines by blending them with others. For example, if you have a wine which has finished too sweet and it cannot be persuaded to ferment any further you can often produce an excellent wine by blending it with a very dry one.

One of the most useful wines for this purpose is a tea wine made rather drier than the recipe I gave in Chapter 5. This also has the advantage of containing a considerable amount of tannin which in most cases helps by adding life to the wine. But if you have one wine which tastes rather vinegary, do not be tempted to try to improve it by blending because it will merely make the final brew taste like vinegar.

While you can blend wines simply by mixing them when they have matured, a far better way is to mix them and then re-ferment so that they develop their new character by producing new alcohol. Mix the two wines together and check the specific gravity; if it shows that there is insufficient sugar to give a satisfactory fermentation add a little more and pour in a yeast starter. The wine should very quickly begin to ferment again and this should be allowed to continue to completion. If you need the wine to be sweeter than it turns out you can always adjust this later by adding a little sugar.

If you know that both wines are fermented out completely and have too much alcohol to allow fermentation to take place mix them and then dilute them with water until you have reduced the alcohol content to enable the new fermentation to take place. If you blend your unsatisfactory wines in this way it will be most unusual if the resulting new wine is not a distinct improvement on either of the original two.

Fortification

In many ways a similar process to blending, fortification is a way of increasing the alcohol content of a wine to make it stronger. It is not possible to produce your wine by normal fermentation with an alcohol content greater than about 18 per cent because at this strength the yeast cells are killed by the alcohol. In order to increase the alcohol content you must add pure alcohol in the form of spirit. This pure alcohol is obtained by distillation which is, of course, illegal for all except those holding a proper excise licence.

The best known commercial fortified wines are Port, Sherry and Madeira together with the Italian and French vermouths and it is possible to produce wines closely resembling these from your home made wines which have been fermented on the appropriate yeasts and made from concentrated grape juice or other fruit bases.

As a general rule, if you ferment your wines to produce as much alcohol as they will, you will end up with a strength of around 18 per cent. To increase this to 20 per cent, which is the average strength of the commercial fortified wines, you need to add about a quarter of a pint of Polish spirit which contains 80 per cent alcohol to the gallon of wine. If you make your basic wine to a somewhat lower alcohol content – say 12 per cent – the quantity of Polish spirit will need to be increased to one pint.

There is a very simple way of working out the correct amount of spirit to be added to a wine to fortify it making use of a device called the Pearson square.

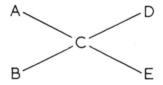

A = the alcohol strength of the fortifying spirit
B = the alcohol strength of the basic wine
C = the strength you want your fortified wine to be
D = the proportion of spirit
E = the proportion of wine

The use of the square is extremely simple. Against A write the strength of the fortifying spirit. If you are using Polish spirit this will be 80 per cent. Against B write the strength of your base wine say, for example, 12 per cent. Against C write the required strength of your fortified wine, say 20 per cent. Now, to find the proportion of the spirit you must add to the wine (D), subtract B from C. This gives in our example 20–12 = 8 and to find the proportion of wine (E), subtract C from A. In this case 80–20 = 60. So for every 60 parts of wine you must add 8 parts of Polish spirit which is roughly one pint of Polish spirit to a gallon of base wine.

In this way you can start with a basic wine of quite modest alcohol content and fortify it to produce a heavy dessert wine of quite considerable strength. But be advised: do not overdo it. Twenty to twenty-two per cent alcohol in a fortified wine is adequate.

Some of the books which I have listed in the bibliography at the end of this book deal in much greater detail with the subject of blending and fortifying wines and if you are interested in this aspect of home wine making I suggest that you read them.

8 Serving your Wine

When you have spent time, money and effort in making wine it makes sense to serve it properly. This is why I suggested that you bottle your wines in proper wine bottles of the type appropriate to the particular wine and why you fit capsules and label it. These seemingly small things all add up to creating a good initial impression when you bring out a bottle of your home made wine to serve it to friends.

Just as important as setting off the wine properly in a bottle is using an appropriate glass. There are all sorts of strange types of glass available on the market, of cut glass, patterned glass, and even (horror of horrors) coloured glass. In my opinion, the simpler the wine glass the better. I prefer to drink my wines − or anybody else's − out of a plain, clear, uncut glass of what is known as the tulip shape. This is a very elegantly shaped glass with the step blending perfectly into the bottom of the bowl which then widens out and narrows again just before the lip. Many people reserve this shape of glass for white wines, but I have found that I can enjoy red wines, white wines, rosés and just about anything from a glass of this classical shape.

An alternative shape for red wines is what is known as a Paris goblet. Like the tulip glass it narrows towards the lip, but the bowl has a much rounder, fuller shape. Both of these glasses allow the bouquet of the wine to develop nicely as long as you do not overfill them; a little more than half full is about right.

For drinking sherry and other dessert wines, there is little to beat the traditional Spanish copita − a smaller glass which again has a bowl which is wide at the bottom, narrowing towards the lip.

Preparing the Wine

When you take a bottle of your wine from the wine rack, treat it very gently so that you do not disturb any sediment which may have been deposited during the storage period. If you have matured your wines properly before bottling them there should be little risk of a sediment, especially with white wines, but it is better to play it safe than to be sorry when you come to drink the wine.

Well designed glasses make drinking wine even more pleasurable. The three shown here are: the classic tulip shape containing white wine; the Paris goblet containing Burgundy; and the Spanish copita for Sherry

If there is any sign of a deposit it is better to decant the wine before serving it; this is a very delicate operation. The ideal way to do it is to use a basket of the type which is often brought to the dining table in restaurants containing your bottle of wine. In actual fact these were never designed for this purpose but simply to hold the bottle at the most suitable angle while decanting a wine, which is what we are now about to do.

Gently draw the cork from the bottle using either a double screw type of corkscrew or one of the lever types. Do not use an ordinary screw-in-and-pull type of corkscrew because you cannot possibly draw the cork using one of these without disturbing the wine and with it any sediment that may be present.

When you have removed the cork, gently lift the basket with the bottle of wine in it and, holding it between your eye and a light source, pour the wine slowly into the decanter. Watch the neck of the bottle very carefully and as soon as you see any sediment begin to cloud the wine, stop pouring. All this applies, though, just to red wines. White wines almost never deposit any sediment after bottling and therefore do not need decanting.

Warm or Cool?

The temperature at which you serve your wine is most important. As a general rule, red wines should be served at room temperature and white wines should be served chilled – and by chilled I do not mean frozen.

Always open a bottle of red wine an hour or two before you intend to serve it and leave it standing in the room where it will be drunk. This enables the wine to absorb oxygen from the air and drives off any remaining metabisulphite smell from the Campden tablets used to preserve the wine during storage. It also has the very beneficial side effect of softening the wine to make it more palatable; this is particularly important if you are drinking a fairly young wine which has not matured to mellowness in the bottle.

Chill your white wines by placing them on the refrigerator door along with the milk for about an hour before serving them. This will cool them sufficiently to be pleasantly refreshing, but will not suppress the bouquet and flavour of the wine. I think it is true to say that more white wines are ruined by over chilling than they

102

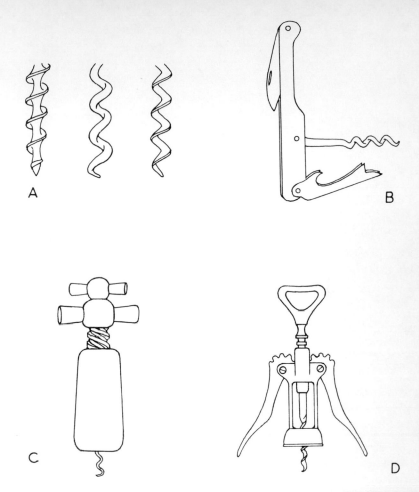

Corkscrews

A   The screw on the left will do little more than pierce the cork, while the sharp edges of the screw on the right may break the cork without actually removing it! The centre screw is rounded; it is easily inserted and will hold the cork firmly, enabling it to be removed without damage

B   This waiter's corkscrew with penknife for cutting metal or plastic capsules also incorporates a 'crown' cork remover

C   Double screw cork extractor. The top lever inserts the screw and the cork is raised by turning the lower lever

D   A butterfly cork extractor. The screw is inserted then the side levers are lowered, pulling the cork out. There is an opener for 'crown' corks on top of the extractor

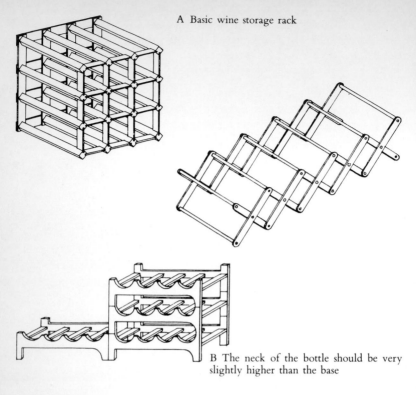

A Basic wine storage rack

B The neck of the bottle should be very slightly higher than the base

C A cardboard carton provides adequate short-term storage

D Wine rack of plastic-coated wire

Wine racks

possibly could be by serving them at room temperature. A white wine chilled in this way makes a really refreshing drink on a hot summer day.

Drinking and eating

Someone — I cannot remember who — once said that a meal without wine is like a day without sunshine. Or something very similar. This is a sentiment with which I heartily agree, because a glass of wine can make even the simplest meal so much more enjoyable. In fact one of my favourite lunches consists simply of French bread, cheese, and a glass or two of Burgundy or home made Burgundy-like wine. But when you come to a more complex meal the balancing of the wine with the food becomes almost an art.

There are general rules which hold good at least until you have established your own opinions on the matter. These are to drink red wine with red meats and white wines with fish and white meats. But as you become more experienced in taking wine with your meals you will begin to establish your own preferences. For example I now prefer to drink a good rich Burgundy with turkey rather than the white wines I used to drink with it.

So really it all boils down to drinking what you like with what you like. As long as *you* enjoy it, who is to say it is wrong?

If you are putting on a real banquet with several courses and you want to serve a different wine with each course, a good general basic rule is to serve a light dry white wine with the starter and fish course, progress to a full bodied red or white wine with the main course and a sweet white Sauterne type with the dessert. Then if you are finishing the meal with cheese, serve a rich red dessert wine such as damson or other port-like wine to accompany it. And if you have a fortified orange, plum or apricot wine you can serve this with coffee to complete the meal.

Drinks for Parties

Traditional party punches and cups are delicious and very easy to make. They are just as good (if not better) made with home-made wines and one of the best is the traditional Spanish punch called Sangria.

Sangria

  1 bottle of good red wine, such as blackberry or damson
  1 glass of brandy
  1 glass of blackcurrant or damson port
  ½pt lemonade
  Chopped fresh fruit — oranges, apples, pears, grapes

Mix all the ingredients in a chilled glass bowl and add several ice cubes.

Fruit cup

You can make a fruit cup with almost any fruit combined with a white wine, preferably of the same type as the fruit you use.

  1 bottle of white wine — apple, apricot, peach, pear, etc
  1 glass of brandy
  2oz caster sugar
  Soda water
  Chopped fresh fruit

Place the fruit in a glass bowl, sprinkle with the sugar, and add the brandy. Do this the day before you intend to drink the fruit cup so that the fruit marinates in the brandy for 12–24 hours. Add the white wine — chilled — dilute with soda water and add ice cubes if you wish.

Store your wine on its side in properly designed racks. This keeps the corks moist and allows any sediment to settle at the bottom of the bottle

Mulled wine

This is a good welcoming drink for your guests especially at Christmas.

½pt water
4oz sugar
4 cloves
1 stick of cinnamon
2 thinly sliced lemons
1 bottle of damson or blackberry wine
1 thinly sliced orange

Boil the water, sugar, cloves and cinnamon together, add the sliced lemons and leave to stand for a quarter of an hour. Add the wine and re-heat, being careful not to boil. Strain into a glass bowl and serve hot with the sliced orange for decoration.

9 Cooking with Wine

That well-known author and gourmet Paul Gallico once made a very profound statement. He said, 'The only difference between cooking with wine and not cooking with wine is that you pour some wine in'. As soon as you mention cooking with wine many people seem to think that it is far too complicated and far too expensive. Nothing could be further from the truth, especially as we have seen that you can make your own wines at a fraction of the cost of the commercial equivalent. If you have not tried cooking with wine and not cooking with wine is that you pour some wine in'. As soon as you mention cooking with wine instance – replace half the liquid which you add to the dish with wine. Red if it is a beef stew, white if it is a chicken casserole. When you eat the dish you will be instantly converted to cooking with wine. And the same applies to beer. If you add beer to a casserole the effect is very nearly as good as adding wine to it.

To give you some ideas to start with, I have collected together a few recipes for dishes which my wife and I often prepare using either commercial or home made wines. They are all very simple to prepare, reasonably inexpensive, and quite delicious. The quantities given are for four servings.

Starters

French onion soup
I think this is my favourite of all soups.

  8oz onions
  $1\frac{1}{2}$oz butter
  1 tablespoon plain flour
  $1\frac{1}{2}$pts beef stock
  $\frac{1}{2}$pt of sherry (use a good one made from grape concentrate)
  Sea salt and freshly ground black pepper to taste
  One thick slice of French bread per person
  Grated Cheddar or Gruyère cheese

Add Sherry type wine to French onion soup . . . delicious!

Chop the onions coarsely while heating the butter in a heavy pan. When the butter is foaming add the onions and cook them gently for about 20 minutes until golden brown, stirring occasionally. Now carefully stir in the flour and cook for a few minutes more. Heat the stock to boiling point. Remove the pan from the heat and pour in the liquid. Add the sherry and seasoning then simmer for about half an hour without a lid on the pan.

While the soup is simmering bake the thick slices of French bread in the oven at around gas mark 4 until they are dry and browned. Place one slice in the bottom of each soup bowl — these should preferably be of the earthenware type with lids — and sprinkle the grated cheese on top. Pour in the boiling soup and place the lids on the bowls and serve immediately. You can have a dish of grated cheese on the table for those who like a little more.

As an alternative starter a pâté is often served. This recipe requires an electric blender.

Chicken liver pâté

8oz chicken livers
3oz butter
1 small onion
Pinch of thyme
1 tablespoon of sherry-like wine
4 rashers plain streaky bacon
1 clove garlic
Sea salt and freshly ground black pepper to taste
1 tablespoon cream

Melt 2oz of the butter in a heavy pan and add the crushed garlic, chopped bacon and onion. Cook gently until they are soft. Add the chopped livers, season and cook gently for about 5 minutes. Allow to cool. Add the cream and sherry and place in an electric blender. Blend until smooth then turn into a serving dish. Smooth the surface and cover with an ounce of melted butter. When cool, place in a refrigerator to chill.

To serve, turn out on to a bed of lettuce and serve with fingers of hot toast and butter.

Main Courses

Pork fillets in Madeira

4 pork fillets
$\frac{1}{2}$ teaspoon sea salt
Freshly ground black pepper
2oz plain flour
4 tablespoons melted butter
4 fluid oz Madeira-type wine
2 fluid oz stock made with a beef stock cube

Place the pork fillets between two sheets of clean plastic or greaseproof paper and flatten with a smooth mallet. Sprinkle them with salt, pepper and flour, shaking off any excess flour. Melt the butter in a large heavy pan and cook the pork fillets on both sides.

Remove them from the pan and keep them warm in the oven. Add the Madeira-type wine to the pan, stirring constantly and mix a tablespoon of the flour for coating the fillets together with the stock. Add these to the pan and cook over a medium heat until the mixture thickens, stirring all the time. Pour this sauce over the fillets and serve with sauté potatoes and courgettes.

Sole in white wine

4 Dover soles
2–2½ tablespoons mixed dried peppers
½pt white wine
1oz butter
2 tablespoons cream

Soak the peppers in the wine for 10 minutes. Wash, fillet and skin the soles and roll up the fillets. Melt the butter in a frying pan, remove from heat, add wine, peppers and the fillets of fish. Bring to the boil and simmer gently for 10 to 15 minutes. When the fish is cooked, put on to a warm dish. Add cream to juices in pan, stir and pour over fish. Serve with creamed potatoes, peas and a slice of lemon

Beef el Dorado

1lb beef chuck steak
2 tablespoons oil
2 small onions, thickly sliced
4 carrots cut in ½in lengths
seasoned flour
½pt light ale
½ tablespoon black treacle
2oz sultanas
salt and pepper

Heat the oil and fry the onions and carrots for 2 minutes. Add the beef, cubed and tossed in the seasoned flour. Fry until the meat is coloured, then pour the ale into the pan and bring to the boil. Add the treacle and sultanas. Cover and cook at gas mark 3, 325°F, for 2½ hours. Serve with natural yoghurt, sprinkled with chopped parsley, and either boiled potatoes or noodles.

Coq au vin gets its characteristic flavour from brandy and a Burgundy type wine

Coq au vin

3oz chopped bacon
6oz mushrooms
4 medium sliced onions
1oz butter
3½lb chicken
4 tablespoons brandy
3 level tablespoons plain flour
½ bottle Burgundy-type wine
¼pt stock

1 tablespoon sugar
Bouquet garni
Sea salt and freshly ground black pepper to taste

Melt the butter in a heavy pan and fry the bacon, mushrooms and onions for a few minutes until lightly browned, then remove them from the pan. Brown the chicken on its breast and underside for about 10 minutes, then pour the brandy over the chicken, remove the pan from the heat and flambé by setting fire to the liquid. When the flames have died down remove the chicken from the pan and place it in a casserole. Stir the flour into the juices in the pan and cook for about 3 minutes, stirring constantly. Add the wine and stock gradually, stirring all the time. Bring to the boil and continue to stir until the mixture thickens. Then add the sugar, bouquet garni and seasoning. Add the bacon, mushrooms and onions to the casserole, pour the sauce over the chicken, cover and cook in a moderate oven (gas mark 4; 360°F) for about an hour. Remove the bouquet garni before serving.

Serve this dish with plain boiled potatoes and a green salad. It is quite superb.

Spaghetti Bolognese

8oz spaghetti
And for the sauce:
2oz chopped bacon
1oz butter
1 large onion, chopped
1 clove garlic, crushed
8oz minced beef
2 tablespoons tomato purée
$\frac{1}{4}$pt dry white wine
$\frac{1}{2}$pt stock made with a beef stock cube
Sea salt and freshly ground black pepper to taste
$\frac{1}{2}$ teaspoon basil
$\frac{1}{4}$ teaspoon powdered nutmeg

Melt the butter in a heavy pan and fry the bacon lightly for 2 to 3 minutes. Add the onion and fry for a further 5 minutes until lightly browned. Add the minced beef and cook until that too is lightly browned. Stir in the tomato purée then add the stock, wine and seasoning. Bring to the boil and simmer with a lid on for about half an hour.

While the sauce is simmering, cook the spaghetti in plenty of boiling salted water. When it is cooked – about 10 minutes – drain it and put a knob of butter in the pan with it. Shake the pan to coat the spaghetti with the butter. Tip the spaghetti on to plates and spoon the sauce over it. Serve piping hot with plenty of Parmesan cheese to sprinkle over the top.

Desserts

Zabaglione

This is a delightful light Italian sweet which is easy to make and will guarantee your success as a host (or hostess).

> 4 egg yolks
> 2oz caster sugar
> ¼pt Sherry or Madeira-type wine

Beat the egg yolks in a basin with the sugar. Then add the Sherry or Madeira and whisk over hot water until the mixture is pale and firm. Serve warm in wine glasses with crisp sponge fingers.

Stuffed baked apples

> 4 cooking apples
> Grated rind of an orange and a lemon
> 4oz sultanas
> 4oz Demerara sugar
> ½pt Sherry or Madeira-type wine
> 4 cloves

Core the apples and stuff them with the sultanas and some of the grated rinds. Place the apples in an ovenproof dish and add the wine, the rest of the rinds, and the cloves. Bake in a moderate oven (gas mark 4; 360°F) for about an hour. Serve with fresh cream.

You can also improve stewed apples beyond all recognition if

Zabaglione is a delicious and simple dessert made simply with eggs, sherry and sugar

you cook them in white wine instead of water.
And finally, a delicacy for Christmas.

Apricots in wine

Buy a pound of the best dried apricots you can find, wash them to remove any preservative, and pack them into Kilner jars. Cover them with a good white wine — I have found a sweetish orange wine is ideal — and leave them to soak for a month or so before Christmas. The taste defies all description. But beware, they are fattening!

Appendix 1

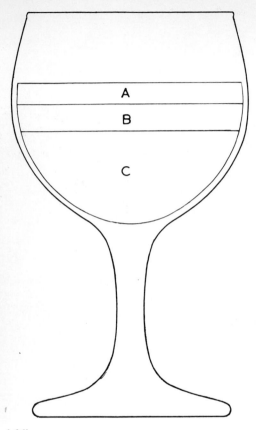

A   Maximum: $\frac{2}{3}$ full
B   Standard: $\frac{1}{2}$ full
C   Suitable for wine tasting: $\frac{1}{3}$ full

Appendix 2

Hydrometer Readings and Potential Alcohol
Content for Various Sugar Contents

Hydrometer Reading	Sugar Content in Gallon	Potential Alcohol
1·010	2oz	0·9%
1·015	4oz	1·6%
1·020	7oz	2·3%
1·025	9oz	3·0%
1·030	12oz	3·7%
1·035	15oz	4·4%
1·040	1lb 1oz	5·1%
1·045	1lb 3oz	5·8%
1·050	1lb 5oz	6·5%
1·055	1lb 7oz	7·2%
1·060	1lb 9oz	7·8%
1·065	1lb 11oz	8·6%
1·070	1lb 13oz	9·2%
1·075	1lb 15oz	9·9%
1·080	2lb 1oz	10·6%
1·085	2lb 4oz	11·3%
1·090	2lb 6oz	12·0%
1·095	2lb 8oz	12·7%
1·100	2lb 10oz	13·4%
1·105	2lb 12oz	14·1%
1·110	2lb 14oz	14·9%
1·115	3lb 0lb	15·6%
1·120	3lb 2oz	16·3%
1·125	3lb 4oz	17·0%
1·130	3lb 6oz	17·7%
1·135	3lb 8oz	18·4%

Appendix 3

Suitable Yeasts for Fruit Wines

FRUIT \ YEAST	NIERSTEINER	HOCK	SAUTERNE	TOKAY	PORT	MADEIRA	BURGUNDY	CHABLIS	SHERRY	BORDEAUX	ZELTINGER	BERNKASTELER	JOHANNISBERGER	ALL-PURPOSE
APPLE	✓	✓	✓					✓			✓	✓	✓	✓
APRICOT	✓	✓	✓	✓							✓	✓	✓	✓
BANANA			✓	✓				✓						✓
BLACKBERRY				✓	✓		✓			✓				✓
BLACKCURRANT					✓		✓							✓
CHERRY			✓	✓		✓	✓			✓				✓
DAMSON					✓		✓			✓				✓
ELDERBERRY				✓	✓		✓			✓				✓
GOOSEBERRY	✓	✓	✓	✓		✓		✓	✓		✓	✓	✓	✓
LOGANBERRY					✓		✓			✓				✓
ORANGE		✓	✓			✓		✓	✓		✓	✓	✓	✓
PEACH	✓	✓	✓	✓				✓			✓	✓	✓	✓
PEAR	✓	✓	✓					✓			✓	✓	✓	✓
PLUM	✓	✓	✓	✓			✓	✓		✓	✓	✓	✓	✓
PRUNE				✓		✓		✓	✓					✓
RHUBARB	✓	✓						✓			✓	✓	✓	✓
RAISIN	✓	✓						✓			✓	✓	✓	✓

Appendix 4

Alcohol Content and Proof Spirit
57·14% alcohol by volume is equal to 100° proof spirit

Alcohol Content (%)	Degrees Proof Spirit
2	$3\frac{1}{2}$
4	7
6	$10\frac{1}{2}$
8	14
10	$17\frac{1}{2}$
12	21
14	$24\frac{1}{2}$
16	28
18	$31\frac{1}{2}$
20	35
22	$38\frac{1}{2}$
24	42
26	$45\frac{1}{2}$
28	49
30	$52\frac{1}{2}$
32	56
34	$59\frac{1}{2}$
36	63
38	$66\frac{1}{2}$
40	70
42	$73\frac{1}{2}$
44	77
46	$80\frac{1}{2}$
48	84
50	$87\frac{1}{2}$
52	91
54	$94\frac{1}{2}$
56	98
58	$101\frac{1}{2}$
60	105

Alcohol Content (%)	Degrees Proof Spirit
62	$108\frac{1}{2}$
64	112
66	$115\frac{1}{2}$
68	120
70	$122\frac{1}{2}$
72	126
74	$129\frac{1}{2}$
76	133
78	$136\frac{1}{2}$
80	140

Appendix 5

Suppliers

Unican Foods Ltd, Central Trading Estate, Bath Road, Bristol
  (Wine and beer kits, concentrates, etc)
Vina (Home Winemaking Supplies) Ltd, 49 Marsh Lane,
  Liverpool
  (Equipment, concentrates, yeasts, etc)
Winecraft, Slate Street, Leicester
  (Equipment, concentrates, yeasts, etc)
Southern Vineyards, Hove, Sussex
  (Equipment, concentrates, yeasts, etc)
Semplex Home Brews Ltd, Old Hall Works, Stuart Road,
  Birkenhead
  (Everything!)
W. R. Loftus, 1–3 Charlotte Street, London W1
  (Everything!)
Home Winemaking Supplies, 12 The Hornet, Chichester, Sussex
  (Wine Kits)
Silverwood Winemakers Stores Ltd, 43 Silverwood Road,
  Millfield, Peterborough
  (3-week wine additive kit)
Itona Products Ltd, Leyland Mill Lane, Wigan
  (Beer kits)
Bar Made Ltd, Mistley, Essex
  (Bag Boy Brewer and other equipment)
Hambleton Bard Ltd, Ornhams Hall, Boroughbridge, Yorks
  (Pressure containers for beer)
Amateur Winemaker Publications Ltd, South Street, Andover,
  Hants
  (*Winemaker* magazine, books, labels, etc)
C. A. Haysom Ltd, 16 Edison Road, Salisbury, Wilts
  (Wine racks)

Further Reading

'Amateur Winemaker' Recipes by C. J. J. Berry (Amateur Winemaker Publications Ltd)

Brewing Better Beers by Ken Shales (Amateur Winemaker Publications Ltd)

The Compleat Home Winemaker and Brewer by B. C. A. Turner (Emblem)

First Steps in Winemaking by C. J. J. Berry (Amateur Winemaker Publications Ltd)

Home Brewed Beers and Stouts by C. J. J. Berry (Amateur Winemaker Publications Ltd)

Making Mead by C. J. J. Berry (Amateur Winemaker Publications Ltd)

Making Wines Like Those You Buy by B. Acton and B. Duncan (Amateur Winemaker Publications Ltd)

The Pan Book of Winemaking by B. C. A. Turner (Pan Books)

The Penguin Book of Home Brewing and Winemaking by W. H. T. Tayleur (Penguin)

Winemaking With Canned and Dried Fruit by C. J. J. Berry (Amateur Winemaker Publications Ltd)

Index

David & Charles have a book on it

Wines for Everyone by L. W. Marrison is a straightforward, practical guide for people with little knowledge of wine. The myths and mystique are dispelled for those who just want to know how to order a wine in a restaurant, or choose something to take home, without the dread of making fools of themselves. At the same time, there is advice for those who would like to go a little further and learn how to appreciate wine in a more informed way, whether or not they have much to spend.

All the well-known table wines – claret, hock, burgundy, moselle, sauternes – are here, and there are also sections on varieties obtainable from all over the world. Illustrated.

The Wines of Germany by Heinrich Meinhard. Heinrich Meinhard was born and raised in Germany and never lost his love of the countryside and people. In this book, he writes with knowledge and affection of the character of the landscape and the buildings of historical interest as well as the wines and produces a companion to the traveller as much as a guide for the wine lover. Illustrated.

The Beer Drinker's Companion by Frank Baillie. Britain is fortunate in having over 1,000 home-produced brands of beer, many of them of great character, but little known and hard to find. This splendid guide introduces the reader to the beers and where to find them. In the course of his researches the author has drunk beer in thirty-six counties. The result is a clear and concise account of the different kinds allied to an informative discussion of many related topics. Illustrated.

A History of Brewing by H. S. Corran is a guide to the technical development of the brewing industry, concentrating mainly on the last 200 hundred years and the changes which led the industry into its present form. Written from the point of view of a technical brewer by someone who has worked for many years at one of the greatest breweries in the world, it is a pioneer effort in its field and should appeal to all serious drinkers. Illustrated.

Scotch: Its History, Distilling and Romance by Ross Wilson. Scotch whisky has a history as long as its popularity today is wide. Try as they may, other countries cannot imitate the unique taste and aroma that comes from the distilleries of Scotland. Only recently has it become an international drink and the biggest export of its country of origin. Ross Wilson, a leading expert on the subject and the author of a classic treatise on Scotch, has now written its history in popular form for for its many consumers who enjoy it but know little of the often jealously guarded secrets and romance that lie behind it. The rich personalities and stories connected with the industry have all been skilfully blended into the story. Illustrated.

Eat Cheaply and Well by Brenda Sanctuary. Rising food prices make this up-to-the-minute book a must for today's housewives. Crammed with sound advice on how to make money stretch further *and* produce elegant dishes for special occasions, it is illustrated by Jon of the *Daily Mail*.

The Home Book of Smoke Cooking by Jack Sleight and Raymond Hull covers the smoking of meat, fish and game. For the inveterate barbecuer, the gourmet and the natural foods enthusiast, a smoke oven is the practical next step in preparing delicious foods right at home, concocted without questionable additives. Smoke-roasting provides a flavour not discovered in ordinary baking, frying or barbecuing. It is practical to perform in the home and is an economical way to make otherwise expensive delicacies. A review of the joys and history of this art, an explanation of the effect of smoke on protein foods, and tips on record keeping to ensure repeated success, pave the way here to an understanding of a nearly forgotten skill.

The Good Cook's Guide by Hilary Fawcett and Jeanne Strang is a selection of recipes from restaurants in the *Good Food Guide*.

Published in association with the Consumers' Association, this successor to the highly successful *Good Food Guide Dinner Party Book* contains over 200 recipes grouped into 18 sections, each dealing with a particular ingredient – apples, dried fruit, garlic, smoked fish, etc. A general introduction to each section provides hints on buying and storing, and ideas for use. Illustrated throughout with attractive two-colour line drawings by Mart Kempers.

Photography books by Derek Watkins

GOOD PHOTOGRAPHY MADE EASY

There can be few homes that do not own a camera of some kind, but most amateur photographers fail to get the best out of their equipment, however simple. Derek Watkins explains how anyone can choose the right kind of camera for the photography that is wanted, and, by observing simple procedures, consistently obtain excellent photographs in colour or black and white. His friendly and straightforward approach to the subject explodes many unnecessary fears about the technicalities of taking pictures. Developing and printing in the home are tackled as an aspect of the hobby that most people deny themselves; anyone can develop and print their own pictures, in colour and black and white, and get maximum enjoyment from photography while saving consider-able sums of money.

210 × 149 mm _____ Illustrated
SLR PHOTOGRAPHY

A Handbook of the Single Lens Reflex

Get more out of your single lens reflex camera with this easy to follow guide presented in three stages. Part one deals with equipment – cameras, lenses and filters; part two covers picture making; part three deals with techniques – exposure meters, choice of films, colour and printing.

247 × 171 mm _____ Illustrated